The Economics of Housing Markets

FUNDAMENTALS OF PURE AND APPLIED ECONOMICS

EDITORS IN CHIEF

J. LESOURNE, Conservatoire National des Arts et Métiers, Paris, France

H. SONNENSCHEIN, University of Pennsylvania, Philadelphia, PA, USA

ADVISORY BOARD

K. ARROW, Stanford, CA, USA
W. BAUMOL, Princeton, NJ, USA
W. A. LEWIS, Princeton, NJ, USA
S. TSURU, Tokyo, Japan

The Fundamentals Series' sections and editors and published titles may be found at the back of this volume.

Further titles in preparation

The Economics of Housing Markets

Richard F. Muth
Emory University, Atlanta, USA

and

Allen C. Goodman
Wayne State University, USA

A volume in the Regional and Urban Economics section
edited by
Richard Arnott
Queen's University, Canada

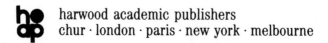
harwood academic publishers
chur · london · paris · new york · melbourne

© 1989 by Harwood Academic Publishers GmbH
Poststrasse 22, 7000 Chur, Switzerland
All rights reserved

Harwood Academic Publishers

Post Office Box 197
London WC2E 9PX
England

58, rue Lhomond
75005 Paris
France

Post Office Box 786
Cooper Station
New York, NY 10276
United States of America

Private Bag 8
Camberwell, Victoria 3124
Australia

Library of Congress Cataloging-in-Publication Data

Goodman, Allen C.
  The economics of housing markets.

  (Fundamentals of pure and applied economics; v. 31. Regional and
urban economics section)
  Bibliography: p.
  Includes index.
  1. Housing—Econometric models. 2. Urban economics.
I. Muth, Richard F., 1927–   . II. Title.
III. Series: Fundamentals of pure and applied economics; v. 31. IV.
Series: Fundamentals of pure and applied economics. Regional and
urban economics section.
HD7287.5.G63 1988   381′.456908   88-31991
ISBN 3-7186-4872-5

TP

Contents

Introduction to the Series

Drawing on a personal network, an economist can still relatively easily stay well informed in the narrow field in which he works, but to keep up with the development of economics as a whole is a much more formidable challenge. Economists are confronted with difficulties associated with the rapid development of their discipline. There is a risk of "balkanization" in economics, which may not be favorable to its development.

Fundamentals of Pure and Applied Economics has been created to meet this problem. The discipline of economics has been subdivided into sections (listed inside). These sections include short books, each surveying the state of the art in a given area.

Each book starts with the basic elements and goes as far as the most advanced results. Each should be useful to professors needing material for lectures, to graduate students looking for a global view of a particular subject, to professional economists wishing to keep up with the development of their science, and to researchers seeking convenient information on questions that incidentally appear in their work.

Each book is thus a presentation of the state of the art in a particular field rather than a step-by-step analysis of the development of the literature. Each is a high-level presentation but accessible to anyone with a solid background in economics, whether engaged in business, government, international organizations, teaching, or research in related fields.

Three aspects of *Fundamentals of Pure and Applied Economics* should be emphasized:

—First, the project covers the whole field of economics, not only theoretical or mathematical economics.

—Second, the project is open-ended and the number of books is not predetermined. If new interesting areas appear, they will generate additional books.

—Last, all the books making up each section will later be grouped to constitute one or several volumes of an Encyclopedia of Economics.

The editors of the sections are outstanding economists who have selected as authors for the series some of the finest specialists in the world.

J. Lesourne   *H. Sonnenschein*

Notation

Greek characters

α, β, γ, δ, η, θ, κ, used to refer to parameters.
ϵ = error term.
λ = Lagrange multiplier.
ξ = random bid.
π = profits.
ρ = discount factor.
σ = non-linear parameter.
σ_e = standard error.
ϕ = probability.
ψ = marginal valuation of time.
$\mu(w)$ = weighted average of factor prices.
Δ = conversion costs.
Φ = cumulative normal distribution function.

English characters

a = private input.
A = parameter.
B = hedonic bids.
c = consumption good.
d, D = demographic variables (vectors).
e = exponential operator.
f = probability of owning.
g = quasi-public good.
g^r = expected rate of capital gain.
h, H = housing services (stock).
ℓ_r = length of residence discount.
L = land.
N, n_i = neighborhood components.
N_p = total population.
n_p = number of households.

O = hedonic price offer.
p = housing price.
r = real rate of interest.
R = land rent.
S = structural components.
SWF = social welfare function.
s_D, S_D = individual (aggregate) housing demand.
s_n = household size.
T = total time.
t_i = marginal tax rate.
t_m = length of residence.
t_r = transactions costs.
U = utility.
u = commuting time.
u_ℓ = time spent working.
u_i, w_i = error terms.
v = vacancy rate.
V = house value.
x = public input.
X = general component.
y, Y^P, Y^T = income.
Z = tenant costs.

Theoretical Issues in Housing Market Research

RICHARD F. MUTH

Emory University, Atlanta, GA, USA

1. INTRODUCTION

Housing is the most important and peculiar of commodities. In the United States about one-seventh of all personal consumption expenditure goes for housing exclusive of household operation and house furnishings. Residential real estate accounts for slightly more than half of the nation's fixed capital stock, and around one-quarter to one-third of gross private domestic investment is made up of residental construction. Mortgage lending has varied from about one-quarter to two-fifths of all funds raised in U.S. credit markets. It is doubtless the case that no item of consumption is so intimately bound up with the lives of individuals as their dwelling unit.

Housing has a variety of characteristics which distinguish it from other commodities. Housing capital, to be sure, is constructed from labor and materials as is any capital good. The consumer satisfactions called housing services, however, are produced almost exclusively by capital and use very little market labor. Housing capital, moreover, is exceptionally durable. New construction averages only about 3 to 3 1/2 per cent per year of the existing stock of housing capital. For these reasons it should not be surprising that new construction of housing is exceptionally sensitive to changes in interest rates and its fluctuations are relatively large as compared with those of other capital goods. Nor should one think it strange that housing demand is substantially affected by changes in house prices as well as by their level.

Housing capital and the services it provides is also heterogeneous and location specific. For these reasons the costs associated with

1

changing one's level of housing consumption are relative large as compared with other commodities. Consequently, long- as opposed to short-term considerations are extremely important insofar as housing demand is concerned. Heterogeneity is thought by many to have especially important implications for housing, though my personal experience suggests that housing is by no means unique in this respect. Locational fixity also means that a dwelling's surroundings are possibly of great importance in affecting its value. Spatial aspects of and externalities in housing, however, are not discussed here.

I have always found it convenient to discuss forces affecting a particular market under the headings of demand and supply and have found housing no different from any commodity in this respect. The second section of this article, therefore, discusses demand aspects of housing markets. The third is concerned with housing supply and market adjustment. The durability of housing implies that housing finance is important enough to be a subject in its own right, and I shall discuss it in Section IV. Finally, in the last section I consider those special theoretical problems associated with the durability and heterogeneity of housing.

The treatment of housing which follows is admittedly idiosyncratic, but hardly original. In the selection of topics and my treatment of them I have been guided almost exclusively by what strikes me as important. I have by no means attempted to write a survey of the literature. I do, however, make reference to some papers which seem to me to provide a useful supplement to what I have discussed. In contrast to the current practice in economics I have tried to make the discussion as readable as possible and have included relatively little mathematics. I have also used this article as an opportunity to set down a few ideas and bits and pieces of technique that I have found useful in thinking about housing but which did not seem to warrant publication by themselves.

2. DEMAND

In this section the determinants of housing demand are considered. Housing is unlike most other commodities in that only one kind of it is typically consumed by a particular household at any one time. For this reason, for many purposes it is desirable to begin the analysis with an examination of the type of housing selected, and I will follow this common practice. The relative price of housing is, as with the analysis of demand for virtually any commodity, a critical determinant of the amount of it which is consumed. Unlike many commodities, for which the nature of the appropriate price variable poses no particular problems, choosing the proper price variable is critical in the analysis of housing demand. The failure to understand the correct housing price variable led even professional economists astray when confronted with a seemingly puzzling performance of U.S. housing markets in the late '70s. Moreover, the exact nature of the income variable in housing demand functions is at least as important a problem as in the aggregate consumption function. I will thus take up the question of price and income variables following the analysis of choice of housing type. Last to be considered is the question of the effect of demographic characteristics, which may feel are of critical importance, on the demand for housing.

At the outset it is critical to be precise about what one means by the term housing. Housing is, in the widest sense, a bundle of many different attributes purchased together. These attributes may contribute to the satisfaction of a variety of different wants, among which are shelter, convenience and social distinction, to use Alfred Marshall's [4] felicitous terminology. For the present I shall follow long established practice by treating housing as if it were a scalar magnitude. Later, in section 5.2, I shall consider the question of whether it is permissible to do so and take up the complications which arise when considering the term housing to mean a vector of attributes. Next, as perhaps the most durable of commodities, one must distinguish between 1) the satisfactions provided by housing per unit of time—the flow of housing services, 2) the stock of assets emitting these services, and 3) the rate of addition to these stocks over time. Correspondingly, one must distinguish between the price of service flows, or rentals, and the price of assets. Finally, it is important to distinguish between the number of bundles of services, or dwelling units, and aggregate or average service flow in talking about the "quantity" of housing either in the sense of service flows or of stocks. Though the law may rightly recognize no distinction between a millionaire's mansion and a pauper's hovel, the two types of dwellings clearly possess different potentials for want satisfaction. For most purposes, quantity in the sense of potential for want satisfaction is clearly more meaningful than quantity as number of dwelling units.

2.1. Type of dwelling

Traditionally, two types of dwellings, rental and owner-occupied housing, have been recognized. For analytical purposes, the distinction is particularly important for issues of housing taxation. Likewise, the decennial Census of Housing in the U.S. has presented separate tabulations and price data for the two tenure types. As interest in the spatial structure of housing markets and in the effect of local governments on these markets developed in recent years, it has become more common to recognize location and municipality along with tenure and perhaps structure type as features which qualitatively distinguish one type of housing from another. The proliferation of housing types and of analyses of choices made among them has also been stimulated, no doubt, by the development of methods for the econometric analysis of qualitative choices. While such methods were clearly appropriate for the study of certain questions in urban transportation for which they were principally developed, their use in the analysis of housing markets is sometimes less clearly motivated.

Let there be I qualitatively different types of housing, q_i be the quantity of housing service per unit time given off by a dwelling of the i-th type and p_i be the rental value per unit of housing service per unit of time for the i-th type, $i = 1, \ldots, I$. Also let a given consumer have the utility function $U_i = U_i(q_i, x)$, where x is dollars of all other consumption per unit time, and the budget constraint be $x + p_i * q_i < = y$. By the usual maximization of utility subject to the budget constraint one obtains functions $q_i = q_i(p_i, y)$, $x = x(p_i, y)$ for each type. Substituting these latter into the utility function one then obtains indirect utility functions $V_i = V_i(p_i, y)$, $i = 1, \ldots, I$. A given consumer (household) then presumably chooses type i over type j if $V_i > V_j$ and type j if $V_j > V_i$ for all $j \neq i$.

The qualitative choice problem becomes an interesting one mainly if one assumes either that a given consumer acts randomly or, alternatively, that different consumers possess different utility functions. Suppose for instance that $V_i = W_i + u_i$; here W_i is either the average utility function for a given consumer or that of the representative consumer, perhaps in some given class, and u_i the random effect of a given instance of choice, having mean zero. Then the probability of choosing type i, $\pi_i = \text{prob}(V_i > V_j) = \text{Prob}(u_j - u_i < W_i - W_j)$, all $j \neq i$. The appropriate statistical model for analyzing such choices depends upon the distribution of the random variable u_i. If the latter has a normal distribution, then the probit model is the appropriate one. Though quite satisfactory for the analysis of dichotomous choices such as that between owning vs. renting, the probit model does not generalize easily to cases involving more than two choices. In such cases it is often assumed that μ_i follows the Weibull distribution, for which $\text{Prob}(\mu_i < \mu) = \exp[-\exp(-\mu)]$. This distribution implies (and is implied by) the logit model,

$$\pi_i = \exp(W_i) \Big/ \sum \exp(w_j),$$

the summation extending over all $j = 1, \ldots, I$. That computational methods for the logit model are now well-developed has no doubt contributed to its recent popularity. (See MacFadden [5] for an excellent discussion of statistical and computational questions inherent in the analysis of qualitative choices.) While I am not aware of any other motivation for using it, I find the tractability of the logit model to be quite compelling.

Though the formal theory of choice among qualitatively distinct types of housing is by now relatively well developed, there has been rather little theoretical analysis of the strategic forces affecting such choices. Tax considerations are obviously important in the choice between owner-occupied and renter housing, and much of the analysis of tenure choice has been motivated by interest in the effects of the personal income tax treatment of income from owner-occupied housing in the U.S. In 1940, however, before federal income tax rates were high enough to be of appreciable importance for the vast majority of U.S. tax payers, about 40 per cent of dwellings in the U.S. were owner-occupied. Thus, I would infer that other important factors influence tenure choice as well.

Principal among these, no doubt, are borrowing costs and the frequency with which a household changes its place of residence.

Historically, houses were purchased with relatively large downpayments, though required downpayments were sharply reduced under the FHA mortgage insurance program introduced during the 1930s and later under the VA mortgage guarantee program in the post World War II period in the U.S. In consequence, the household's accumulated non-human wealth is certainly one of the important factors affecting tenure choice. Another is the rate of interest paid on loans relative to those paid by owners of rental property. These rates are high relative to mortgage rates for households who borrow to finance the purchase of automobiles or other consumer durables or have incurred indebtedness under unsecured personal loans. Finally, in addition to the cost of transporting one's possessions to a new location and the non-pecuniary costs of changing one's residence, the transactions costs associated with buying and selling a home may well be of the order of 10 per cent of the sales price of a house. Consequently, for households who move frequently homeownership is expensive relative to renting. All the factors just enumerated doubtless help explain relatively low home-ownership rates among lower-income and younger households.

Factors affecting residential location choice have received extensive study in recent years. Since these are treated in another work in this series I will comment only briefly on them here. Workplace location, certainly, is one of the critical factors affecting the choice of residential location because of the costs of commuting. In most cases of interest, however, the number of households with a member working in some particular location is large relative to the number of residences adjacent to it. Consequently, such households must locate in an area surrounding it which is large relative to that of the workplace itself. Moreover, in market equilibrium identical households in different locations relative to a common workplace must be equally well-off or achieve the same level of utility. The question of genuine interest, then, is how the spatial pattern of rental values of housing varies so as to make households indifferent as among alternative residential locations surrounding this common work-place. One would not expect that the question of why any given household chose its particular location to yield any interesting information in such cases.

Matters are quite similar insofar as factors associated with local government are concerned. Suppose, for example, that a particular community provides a better than average school system at a given tax price to residents of that community. Presumably, households which place above average value on public education will find residences in that community to be attractive. The number of such households in an urban area, however, is certainly large relative to the size of a single suburban community. In market equilibrium, again, households of a given type must be indifferent to locating in the community in question and others. As a result, land rentals or the rentals of residential sites plus the fixed structures on them must be sufficiently higher in this particular community to offset the advantages of the local public schools. That the local public schools are of particular high quality will say little of interest about the choices made by households locating in the community. Rather, to analyze the impact of the public schools and similar local governmental variables, one might better look at their relation to the rental values of residential real estate in different communities.

2.2. Price

In everyday discourse, the term 'housing price' simply means the amount paid for a particular dwelling. It is used to refer either to the rental value of tenant-occupied dwellings or to the purchase price of owner-occupied ones. As was indicated earlier, however, the flow of services from an asset and the asset itself are conceptually quite distinct. Moreover, if units adjacent to each other rent or sell for quite different amounts, it is unreasonable to attribute these differences to differences in price. Rather, such differences arise because of differences in the amount or quantity of housing these dwellings represent. For analytical purposes, it is best to reserve the terms rental and price for the amount per unit of housing service.

When analyzing the demand for housing services, the rental paid per unit of housing service is the obvious choice of a "price" variable for renter housing. What is the appropriate variable for owner-occupied housing? The simplest answer to this question can be given by considering a home-owner who buys a house from himself (to avoid the problem of transactions cost when dealing with others) at relative price P and resells it to himself $1/n$th year later at price $P(1 + r/n)$, where r is the annual rate of increase of house prices over the interval. During the interval he incurs maintenance costs at rate m and the quantity of housing services given off declines or depreciates at rate d, both measured in annual rates. Where q is the initial size of the dwelling, measured by the rate of flow of housing services given off, and neglecting taxes, the budget constraint facing the owner-occupier is

$$x + (m/n)Pq = y - Pq + P[(1 + r/n)(1 - d/n)/(1 + \rho/n)]q$$

where x is dollars of expenditure on all other consumption, y the home-owner's real income and ρ the rate at which he discounts the future. Rearranging,

$$x + P[1 + m/n - (1 + r/n)(1 - d/n)/(1 + \rho/n)]q = y.$$

The coefficient of q on the left has been called the user-cost or the implicit rental value, R, of owner-occupied housing. Expressing R in terms of its annual rate and letting n become arbitrarily large, the instantaneous implicit rental rate is simply $R = P(\rho + d + m - r)$. Quite similar results are found in an explicit multi-period model or in a continuous optimization over time, namely that the household adjusts its consumption in each period or at each moment to the implicit rental value per unit of housing service.

Apart from tax considerations, then, the implicit rental rate or price of housing services to a home-owner is the asset price per unit of housing service multiplied by the gross rate of return on housing, g. The latter is the sum of interest, depreciation and maintenance costs per dollar of asset value less the rate of appreciation of house prices, or capital gains. That the asset prices of houses were rising rapidly in the late '70s provides the key to the apparent paradox of high asset prices and eager buyers, many of them younger or first time home-owners. Houses, though highly priced, were then relatively cheap to live in, as many calculations have shown, because of the capital gains accruing to home-owners during this time. Quite similar considerations apply when analyzing the alleged "crisis" in rental housing during the '70s. Real rental values were indeed declining during the decade, but such declines were probably offset by appreciation in asset values. Competition among owners of rental property would have kept rentals at the level indicated by a similar expression for the user cost of rental housing. Note also that the distinction between housing for consumption and for investment of which some have written is seen to be artificial by the above development. The user cost of housing as consumption is necessarily affected by its appreciation as an investment. Maximization of the utility function $U = U(x, q)$ subject to the budget constraint developed two paragraphs above yields the demand for housing services function $q = q(R, y)$. The stock or asset demand function, like that of any productive factor, is derived, in part, from this output demand function. It is commonly assumed for simplicity that the rate of flow of housing services, q, is numerically equal to the stock of the asset providing this flow, Q. (Some modifications to this last assumption will be considered in section 3.1). The stock demand function for housing is then $Q = Q(P, g, y)$. Thus, any of the factors affecting the gross rate of return on housing, g, cause the stock demand function for housing—viewed as a relation between asset price P and quantity of stock demand—to shift. A rise in the rate of interest, for example, though leaving the demand for the flow of housing services unchanged, by increasing the gross rate of return on housing will cause the stock demand curve for housing to shift downward and to the right. In similar fashion, an increase in the instantaneous rate of appreciation in house prices will lead to an upward shift in the stock demand for housing, given the position of the demand schedule for housing services.

So far the analysis has neglected the fact that households sometimes move from one dwelling to another. Moving is of special interest because of transaction costs. Their existence in effect means that when moving the budget constraint facing a consumer lies inside that which obtains if the consumer remains in the same residence. This reduction in resources may be more than counter-balanced by allocating remaining resources more efficiently as between housing and other items of consumption. Several examinations of this problem have convinced me that it is not very fruitful of interesting implications. It seems not unreasonable, however, to view moving costs as so large that moves are made only in certain rare circumstances, such as changing the nature of the household due to death or divorce or to large changes in place of employment. Such changes might be interpreted as random events, and the household might be viewed as maximizing expected utility over an uncertain duration of tenure in a particular dwelling.

In doing so, the budget constraint facing a household is its expected wealth, w, at the end of its occupancy of the dwelling to be chosen at time $t = 0$. For a duration of occupancy of t years, wealth at the end of the period is

$$w(t) = \int_o^t [y(v) - x(v) - mP(v)d(v)q_0]\exp(-\rho v)dv - P_0 q_0$$
$$+ P(t)d(t)q_0\exp(-\tau t),$$

where q_0 is the initial rate of flow of housing services from the dwelling selected and $d(t)$ is the depreciation function relating the flow at time t to the initial rate. If the density function for length of stay in the dwelling is $f(t)$, then expected wealth over the duration of occupancy is

$$E(w) = \int_o^T w(t)f(t)\, dt$$
$$= Y - X - \left\{ P(0) + M - \int_o^T P(t)\, d(t)\exp(-\rho t)f(t)\, dt \right\}q_0,$$

where T is the maximum length of occupancy, perhaps time to retirement. Here Y is the expected present value of income to be received during the period of occupancy of the dwelling

$$\int_o^T \left[\int_o^t y(v)\exp(-\rho v)\, dv \right] f(t)\, dt.$$

Future incomes are here presumed to be known with certainty; uncertainty attaches only to length of occupancy of the current dwelling and whether income to be received t years from now is relevant to the current housing decision. X is similarly defined as the expected present value of expenditure on consumption other than housing and M the expected present value of maintenance expenditures during occupancy of the dwelling

$$m\int_o^T \left[\int_o^t P(v)\, d(v)\exp(-\rho v)\, dv \right] f(t)\, dt.$$

The "price" term in the budget constraint is seen to be the initial purchase price plus the expected present value of maintenance expenditures over the uncertain period of occupancy less the expected present value of the dwelling at the uncertain date of moving from it.

Following the analysis in Muth [11], the optimizing consumer equates the price term just described to

$$\int_o^T \int_o^t (Uq/Ux)\, d(v)\exp(-\rho v)\, dv]f(t)\, dt.$$

This last is the expected discounted present value of the marginal rate of substitution of housing for other consumption over the period the household resides in it. Here discounting accounts not only for the phenomenon of interest but also for depreciation. In particular, if the rate of flow of housing services declines over time because of depreciation and/or the household's income increases during its period of occupancy, the dwelling it occupies will be too large early in its occupancy and too small in latter years. Though in equilibrium on the average, in the sense described earlier, the analysis implies that households who have recently moved will occupy larger dwellings and spend more on housing than otherwise identical households who have occupied their dwellings for a longer period of time. Other and I think more interesting implications of the analysis just described will be discussed in subsequent parts of this section. It should be possible, of course, to allow for uncertainty in future income levels or future asset prices for housing along similar lines. It is uncertain, however, whether doing so would yield interesting empirical implications.

2.3. Income

It has long been recognized that quite different relationships are found between total consumption expenditure and current income when examining data for individual consumer units at a given point of time on the one hand and aggregate consumption and income over widely separate periods of time on the other. In the former case, consumption invariably appears to increase less rapidly than income, while in the latter it would appear that roughly a constant fraction of income appears to be consumed. Many, if not most, economists would accept some version of the permanent income or of the life cycle hypothesis in order to reconcile the apparent divergent behavior reflected in the two kinds of data.

Much the same is the case regarding the relation of housing expenditure to income. In virtually any set of cross section data for individual consumer units, the fraction of income spent on housing would appear to decline as income increases. On the other hand, aggregate time-series data for the U.S. as a whole give a much different relationship. Space rental expenditures for housing relative to disposable personal income from the national income and product accounts suggest that the fraction of income spent on housing in the late 1970s was almost identical with the ratio for 1929. To be sure, the ratio increased in the early 1930s and declined until the late 1940s. It subsequently rose until the early 1960s and has remained remarkably constant since that time. Beginning with Margaret Reid's [12] pioneering work, many have argued that the relation of housing expenditure to permanent income is more stable than that to current income. Indeed, if one calculates housing expenditure in relation to income, both in real terms, from data in successive decennial censuses of housing and plots them, an almost text book illustration of the permanent income hypothesis is found.

Given these elementary empirical considerations, it is remarkable how little attention has been paid to the appropriate income variable in theoretical, or for that matter many empirical, analyses of housing demand. On the one hand, it is by no means clear that an appropriate long-run measure of income is income averaged over a period of two or three years. On the other hand, however, it is by no means obvious that some expectation over the whole of one's life-cycle is the appropriate measure either. To take but one example, university students living off-campus almost certainly have better dwellings than others of the same current money income receipts, but they rarely occupy as good or better quarters than their parents, as some forms of the life-cycle hypothesis would imply.

An hypothesis which suggests an income measure intermediate between those of some forms of the permanent income and life-cycle hypotheses is that suggested in the previous part of this section. This asserts that, when moving, consumers maximize expected utility subject to an expected wealth constraint, where both expectations are taken over an uncertain duration of stay in a given dwelling. As was indicated above, the income measure suggested by this analysis is the expected value of discounted income over the period of occupancy of a given dwelling. The expression given earlier may be written as

$$Y = \int_o^T y(t) \left[\int_t^T f(v) \, dv \right] \exp(-\rho t) \, dt.$$

Thus income to be received in t years is discounted not only at whatever interest rate is appropriate for the household but also by the probability that the household does not move for t years. In this regard, for households which move frequently the appropriate measure of permanent income might well be average income over the next two or three years. For others, incomes expected over the whole life cycle might be appropriate. As an example of this last, I have known several instances of physicians who, while first establishing a practice and equipping offices, have purchased houses which were large relative to those of more mobile contemporaries. At the same time, among Army officers living in off-base housing, lieutenants almost invariably inhabit smaller quarters than, say, majors and majors smaller quarters than generals.

2.4. Demographic characteristics

One of the oldest assertions in the field of housing economics is that new construction is closely related to household formation. When one realizes, however, that a household is defined as that collection of persons which inhabits a dwelling unit, it is not surprising that increases in the one should be closely related to increases in the other. In empirical studies of tenure choice, considerable attention has been given to demographic characteristics such as age of household head, race and number of children. Less frequently have studies of housing consumption or expenditure paid attention to such household characteristics. To my knowledge there has been virtually no theoretical study of the affects of family composition on housing consumption, although the literature abounds in such insightful statements as 'families with children prefer more bedrooms and large yards.'

There is considerable causal evidence which suggests that the number and kind of collections of persons inhabiting separate quarters is importantly influenced by economic factors. Those of us who are old enough will recall numerous instances of younger married couples who lived in one parents' dwelling during the period of rent controls following World War II. More recently, with the maturing of the baby boom generation of the 1950s it was widely predicted that a boom in multi-family construction would occur during the 1970s. In fact, as the rental values of owner-occupied dwellings declined relative to those of rental units during the past decade in the U.S., the fraction of rental units declined as did the average age of home buyers. It is much less common today to see one or both parents of a husband or wife living with their married children than it was a half century ago, while at the same time young adults move to separate dwellings much more frequently. A recent study by Smith et al. [15] has documented the importance of housing rentals and income as determinants of the non-family household headship rate.

An increase in the number of non-family households leads to an increase in the demand for housing as dwelling units. At the same time, with smaller households the quantity of housing services per dwelling doubtless decreases. Whether the total stock of housing increases or decreases as the number of households in a given population changes depends upon which of the two forces is the stronger. It may well be the case that the total number of bedrooms is unaffected by the manner in which a given population is divided up into households. On the other hand, there may well be economies of scale in the provision of facilities for cooking, bathing and watching television within a household. If such is the case, the division of a given population into a larger number of households might well be associated with an increase in the aggregate demand for housing services. As a corollary one would anticipate that the price and income elasticities of the stock demand per capita would be numerically larger than those of the stock demand per household.

Some evidence suggests that both younger and older households, as defined by the age of head, tend to spend larger amounts on housing than do households with middle-age heads. For younger households this may be partly explained by life cycle income effects. The money income receipts of younger workers tend to increase more rapidly than do those of middle-aged and older workers. Consequently, since households tend to remain in a given dwelling for a period of some years because of moving costs, average income over the expected period of occupancy is larger given current income for a younger household. Younger households will also have typically lived in their current dwelling for a shorter period of time. If size of dwelling tends to decline relative to the optimal level determined by current income over the period of occupancy of a dwelling, younger households will tend to spend more on housing given current income on this account as well. For households approaching retirement age, however, the expected period of occupancy of any given dwelling is smaller than for a younger household. In effect, the price of housing is smaller for older households for this reason, and they consequently spend more on housing at current income levels. (For an elaboration see Muth [11]).

3. SUPPLY AND MARKET ADJUSTMENT

Housing is probably the most long-lived of all durable goods. Net additions are rarely more than 3 to 3 1/2 per cent of the current stock. Thus, at any moment in time the stock of housing inherited from the past largely determines the amount of accommodation currently available. Moreover, housing depreciates quite slowly over time. Estimates of the rate of depreciation range from perhaps 1/2 to 2 per cent per year. In part, differences in these estimates depend upon the notion of housing studied. In purely physical terms, with normal maintenance there may be little or no diminution in the capacity of a dwelling to satisfy wants. Dwellings may well obsolesce, however, for as incomes and thus the quantity of housing services demanded per dwelling increase over time, the rental offered for a unit of any given size may well decrease after some time. That few log cabins are in use today may merely reflect the fact that no one wants to live in them, even though they might have supplied very nearly the same absolute amount of want satisfaction as when originally built.

Though in highly inelastic supply over very short periods, new construction and depreciation/obsolesence allow for considerable variation in the housing stock over moderately long time periods. Construction at a net rate of 3 1/2 per cent per year adds 40 per cent to the stock of housing over a decade. Conversely, a cessation of home building would allow the stock to decline by 5 to almost 20 per cent over the same period of time. Over such longer periods, then, the elasticity of the supply of housing depends principally upon the supply elasticity of new construction. In this section, I shall first consider the determinants of the supply of new construction. I shall then turn to an examination of housing market equilibrium and to the process of adjustment of an equilibrium position. Finally, I will consider the impact of a variety of regulations which are said to limit the supply of housing and suggest methods for analyzing the impacts of such limitations.

3.1. Supply of new construction

Houses are built using a variety of materials and different types of construction labor. As is the case with non-residential structures and equipment, it is convenient to treat the embodiment of these resources in completed dwellings as capital, K. (A rationale for doing so is discussed in the following paragraph.) Land, L, is also an important input into the production of housing. Not only does land provide a place to put the capital embodied in a structure, but it also serves as a direct source of want satisfaction, in providing space for certain recreational activities, for example, Outside of agriculture, urban housing is probably the greatest single user of land, accounting for perhaps two-fifths of all developed urban land. Moreover, transportation, much of which is directly derived from residential demand, uses another quarter or so of urban land. Finally, the flow of housing services from a particular structure is dependent upon the amount of current expenditure for heating and other utilities as well as the amortization of furnishing and equipment for cooking, heating, etc.

Consider, first, the provision of residential structures. For many purposes, the relative prices of construction labor and materials are more or less constant. Indeed, when considering the housing market of some particular metropolitan area, even more so for a small part of such an area, it would seem likely that the supply functions for both labor and for materials are highly elastic ones. Consequently, by the composite-commodity theorem the aggregate called capital responds as a single factor input. One's first thought, perhaps, is that the supply of land is also highly elastic, for in most urban areas the opportunity cost of land in farming is unlikely to depend appreciably on the area's size. An expansion in the urban area limits, however, leads to an increase in the cost of commuting from its outermost part to the downtown part of the area. The latter increase amounts to very much the same thing as an upward sloping supply curve for urban residential land. Moreover, to the extent that a unique agricultural product is grown surrounding a city—wine grapes in certain parts of the San Francisco Bay area, for example, the supply curve of residential land may be upward sloping on this account as well. Finally, for a small part of some urban area the supply of land may well be highly inelastic, especially so over moderately short periods of time when non-residential uses of land are fixed.

It is usually assumed that housing is produced under conditions of constant returns to scale. Such an assumption seems quite reasonable so long as the average size of dwelling is fixed and one is concerned principally with expansion in the number of units. Because of possible indivisibilities in providing certain housing attributes such as sanitary and cooking facilities, however, increasing returns to scale might possibly prevail over certain ranges of dwelling sizes. Given constant returns to scale, the supply curve of structures to an urban area or to one of its parts depends, of course, on the elasticities of supply of capital, as defiend in the paragraph above, and land. Where, as in this instance, these supply elasticities differ, the elasticity of structure supply also depends upon the relative importance of these two factors and upon their elasticity of substitution in production.

The fraction of new, FHA-insured house values accounted for by land remained remarkably stable at about one-fifth during the '70s. When one realizes, however, that the above figure refers to developed sites and that the latter includes the value of capital improvements at least equal to raw land value itself, the latter's share in production is probably of the order of 10 per cent. It seems clear on the basis of purely causal observation that considerable substitutability between capital and land exists in the production of structures. Quite different relative amounts are embodied in downtown elevator apartments, on the one hand, and in surburban ranch houses on the other. It is probably the case, however, that the fraction of structure value attributable to land is higher in the former instance. Moreover, what data are available suggest that the fraction of structure values attributable to land is about twice the national average in coastal areas of California, where per square foot land values are especially high. It would thus seem that the elasticity of substitution of capital for land in producing structures is certainly less than one. Most empirical estimates tend to support this inference; these have found values which average perhaps 0.75.

In the short run, the supply of housing services depends both upon the fixed stock of residential structures and upon current inputs purchased by producers of housing. Like most kinds of building materials, it seems highly probable that fuel for heat and light as well as furnishings and equipment are in highly elastic supply to a given urban area. Thus, again appealing to the composite commodity theorem it seems reasonable to treat current inputs or expenditure on them as a single aggregate, C. In the aggregate, current inputs account for perhaps one-quarter of the total cost of providing housing services, and it would appear that the degree of substitution between current inputs and structures is very low. The precise nature of the short run supply curve of housing services—which is the sum of the marginal cost curves of all housing producers—depends critically upon the functional form of their production functions. For a constant elasticity of substitution (CES) function in structures, S and current inputs, C, it is not difficult to show that marginal cost is very flat for small outputs but approaches the vertical for large enough outputs per unit of structure (see Muth [9]). On the other hand, it is even easier to show that for a displaced Cobb-Douglas (DCD) function

$$Q = S^{\alpha}(C + \beta S)^{1-\alpha},$$

whose elasticity of substitution is less than unity for $\beta < 0$, marginal cost increases log-linearily with Q/S.

In the long run, of course, the stock of residential structures is variable. The production function for housing services underlying the supply function for housing services then includes capital, land, and current inputs as separate arguments. If the relative prices of capital and current inputs are fixed, however, it is convenient to combine them into a single aggregate N, i.e., non-land factors. The elasticity of supply of housing services then depends upon the relative importance of land, the substitutability of non-land factors for land, and upon the elasticity of supply of land. Because, as was noted earlier, land's share is relatively small and land and capital are relatively substitutable for each other, the supply elasticity of housing services is likely to be relatively large. On the assumption that the supply elasticity of non-land factors is arbitrarily large, one can show from 1) the production function, 2) the marginal conditions for income maximization of producers and 3) the supply function for land that the elasticity of supply of housing services, e, is equal to

$$(k_N \sigma + e_L)/k_L$$

where $k_N (= 1 - k_L)$ is the relative importance of non-land inputs and σ is the elasticity of substitution of non-land inputs for land. For $k_L = 0.1$ and $\alpha = 0.75$, e varies from about 7 to 15 as e_L varies from 0 to 1.

3.2. Market equilibrium and adjustment to it

The determination of housing market equilibrium is a relatively simple process when concerned only with the determination of price in the short-run, in which the housing stock is given by the past. In such a situation, fluctuations in the demand for housing lead only to changes in housing prices. Specifically, let

$$Q_d = a_0 - a_1 * P + a_2 * dP/dt,$$

where Q_d is housing stock demanded and considerations other than price, including the rate of interest, taxes, and any factors shifting the demand for housing services are impounded in the constant term. The rate of change in price over time affects stock demand through its effect upon the gross rate of return on housing stocks. Making the standard assumption that the rate of change in price is proportional to the excess of quantity demanded over quantity supplied—here the existing housing stock,

$$dP/dt = b * (Q_d - Q).$$

Upon substituting and solving,

$$dP/dt = a_0' - a_1' * P - b' * Q,$$

where, for example, $a_1' = ba_1/(1 - ba_2)$.

Equilibrium, of course, requires that $dP/dt = 0$; letting P_e be the market equilibrium price and $P' = P - P_e$, the differential equation defining the trajectory of price becomes

$$dP'/dt = -a_1 * P',$$

whose solution, of course, is

$$P' = \Gamma * \exp(-a_1' t).$$

The actual market price will then converge to its equilibrium value regardless of initial conditions if $a_1' > 0$. The latter will hold if $b < 1/a_2$, that is, so long as the rate of adjustment of price over time is not too rapid. If the rate of price adjustment is less than this critical value, a faster adjustment of price over time increases the rate at which the market returns to equilibrium.

Over longer periods of time when the stock of housing may change with new construction, depreciation of the existing stock, and perhaps, with other factors, one must also define the rate of change of the housing stock as well. The simplest hypothesis, probably, is

$$dQ/dt = c_0 + c_1 * P - d * Q.$$

Here, the first two terms represent the supply function for new units of stock, with any factors other than price, such as construction costs, implicit in the constant term. The last term is depreciation of the existing stock, which is substracted to arrive at net additions to the housing stock. Letting Q_e be the equilibrium stock and $Q' = Q - Q_e$ in a manner similar to price in the above paragraph, one now has a system of two simultaneous differential equations

$$dP'/dt = -a_1' * P' - b' * Q'$$
$$dQ'/dt = c_1 * P' - d * Q'.$$

The solutions to such a system, of course, are given by expressions

$$\Gamma_1 \exp(\lambda_1 t) + \Gamma_2 \exp(\lambda_2 t),$$

where the characteristic roots of the system are given by

$$\lambda = [-(a_1' v + d) \pm ((a_1' + d)^2 - 4(a_1' d + b' c_1))^{1/2}]/2.$$

Provided that both roots have negative real parts, P and Q converge to their equilibrium values regardless of the initial conditions of the housing market. Sufficient conditions for such stability are

$$a_1' + d > 0 \quad \text{and} \quad a_1'd + b'c_1 > 0.$$

Since d is small, the former is essentially the condition for static stability. The latter is readily seen to be identical to the usual condition that the slope of the equilibrium stock supply function, c_1/d, be greater numerically than that of the stock demand function, $-a_1'/b'$.

Even though the stability conditions just discussed are satisfied, the housing market may behave in a somewhat unexpected way. If $P' > 0$ and $Q' > 0$ but not too much so, then the stock of housing may continue to grow for a time until stock prices have fallen sufficiently. Once this has occurred, stock will decline toward its equilibrium level before returning to this level. Such can occur even though both characteristic roots are real, so that asymptotically the market decays monotonically to its equilibrium. Alternatively, suppose that $Q' < 0$, $P' > 0$ but not too much so. Then price will first rise further before returning to its equilibirum level. Finally, even though both λ's have negative real parts, if $(a_1' + d)$ is sufficiently small as compared with $b'c_1$ these roots are complex. In this event, the long-run adjustment of the housing market will be oscillatory.

The implicit rental value of a unit of housing stock $R = (\rho + d + m - r)$, moreover, behaves in a somewhat unexpected manner. Suppose, for example, that the market rate of interest rises sharply, as it did in 1979 and the early '80s. If housing markets were previously in equilibrium, the result will be a sharp rise in R. Since the rise in ρ causes a downward shift in the stock demand curve for housing, P begins to fall; $dP/dt < 0$ causes R to increase further. The fall in P reduces the excess of the current stock over stock demanded so that dP/dt becomes numerically smaller. The latter together with the lower value of P itself first moderates the increase in R and later causes R to decline toward its old equilibrium level, provided of course that the market is stable. Similarly, if the stock demand for housing increases, R will fall sharply and continue to fall for a time before returning to its equilibrium.

When considering rental housing, one must also consider the behavior of market rental levels. It is frequently alleged that because of the existence of long-term leases or perhaps other reasons market rentals are slow to adjust over time. Thus, if for some reason the demand for the services of rental housing were to decline, an excess supply of rental accommodation would exist at previous rental levels. The resulting excess supply would presumably cause rentals to begin to decline. The decline in rentals, in turn, would cause the excess supply to diminish, slowing the decline in rentals. Ultimately, if the rental market were stable rentals would adjust to the new equilibrium. The findings of some empirical studies are consistent with the process just described. Others, however, have failed to find any association between rental levels and vacancies, and their authors have expressed doubts about the adjustment of rentals to an excess supply of rental accommodations.

Vacancies, of course, vary inversely with excess supply, just as unemployment varies with excess supply in labor markets. And, in a manner similar to assertions once made regarding labor markets, there is a tendency in the literature on rental markets to argue that rentals are rigid so long as housing markets are "slack" and adjust upward only when these markets become "tight." A much more satisfactory interpretation, it seems to me, would be to recognize, as labor economics has come to do over the past decade, that for any market there is a "natural" or equilibrium level of vacancies. The natural level may vary considerably among markets, depending upon their particular characteristics. Among the more important of these is the growth in housing demand in the market in question. Indeed, vacancy rates have been relatively high in rapidly growing areas for the past decade or so. In such areas, presumably, newly constructed units are a larger fraction of the housing stock, and new units are typically vacant for a period between their completion and first occupancy. Moreover, in areas where a larger fraction of the population are new residents, movement from one residence to another may well be more frequent. When moves from one residence to another occur, units are vacant for a time, of course. Conversely, where a housing market is growing more slowly, the natural vacancy rate may well be smaller.

Also along lines similar to those currently employed in the analysis of labor markets, at rental levels above the market equilibrium level vacancies will tend to exceed the equilibrium or natural level. Likewise, at rentals below the market equilibrium level, vacancies will tend to be smaller than normal. Excess supply will be related not to the absolute level of vacancies but will rather vary inversely with the excess of the actual vacancy rate over the equilibrium level. The rate of change of rentals over time will as well vary inversely with the excess of the actual over the equilibrium level. Any comparison of rental levels or their change over time with the actual level of vacancies among different housing markets will be misleading because of the omitted natural vacancy rate variable. For this reason I am inclined to suspect the results of studies which claim to have demonstrated that the adjustment of rentals is not associated with vacancy rates. The rate of change of rentals would vary inversely with actual and directly with equilibrium vacancies, and the two rates would tend to be positively correlated. The coefficient of actual vacancies when equilibrium vacancies are omitted would thus be upward biased.

3.3. Limitations on housing supply

Complaints have long been voiced that zoning restrictions, building codes and above market wages secured for their members by building trades unions have raised housing costs in the U.S. During the past decade and a half, local governments have shown considerable ingenuity in developing new kinds of restrictions on housing. Among these are a variety of growth controls, inclusionary zoning, rent controls and limitations on the conversion of rental units to condominium ownership. During this same period, as house prices soared, many of these restrictions have been charged with contributing to increased housing costs. In what follows, I wish to discuss the effect of some of these restrictions and indicate how one might determine their impact on housing asset prices and rentals.

Before discussing the various kinds of restrictions themselves, however, one introductory comment is necessary. The impact to any of these restrictions depends critically upon the nature of the governmental unit imposing it. If a small local government in some urban area imposes such a restriction by itself, the principal impact of the restriction may merely be to divert residential investment to neighboring communities with but negligible overall impact on the urban area as a whole. Though the effect may be substantial within the community imposing the restriction itself, it would be mistaken to suppose that the effects are similar thoughout a wider area. In only a few areas, especially those in which county governments exercise regulatory powers most usually employed by municipalities, would the effects of such restrictions be substantial. Examples of such urban areas in the U.S. are the Atlanta and Washington, D.C. areas. In many others, however, regulation of housing and land-use is the responsibility of much smaller jurisdictions.

The term zoning strictly refers to regulations which limit the types of economic activity, especially single- and multi-family residential, commercial and industrial, that can be undertaken in various parts of a jurisdiction. It has been broadened in popular usage, however, to include a wide variety of restrictions. Zoning restrictions are usually justified on the ground of preventing external effects on surrounding land-uses. What is not often recognized, however, is that the market itself will tend to produce disjointed clusters of unlike land-users where such external effects are important. Indeed, it has been observed (see Siegan [14]) that in Houston, Texas, the only large U.S. city without zoning, the clustering of unlike land-uses predominates in much the same way as in other U.S. cities. To the extent that zoning regulations have a valid role to play in achieving economic efficiency, they should be directed principally at regulating the relative sizes of different areas of land-use.

Included in the narrower meaning of zoning are limitations on the amount of land for multi-family residential developments below that which the unregulated market itself would produce. Reports of large gains to be had from rezoning single- to multi-family use lend some credence to assertions that such reductions in fact occur. There are grounds, however, for doubting that such reductions do occur. In the first place, if gains are to be had from re-zoning rational political action would tend to permit it and to extract compensation for the community at large rather than prevent it. In addition, it is by no means clear that owners of single family structures can obtain land more cheaply by supporting such restrictions, for in the long-run land prices to them are fixed by non-urban land costs at the urban area's edge. Moreover, if truly restrictive, developers would seek to set up separate communities where unrestricted multi-family development would be permitted, and to my knowledge such communities do not exist. If effective, however, zoning restrictions would reduce the supply elasticity of land for multi-family structures and raise the asset prices of such structures.

The effects of any one of a variety of controls limiting the number of new dwellings built during any year would be similar to those just discussed. At the limits imposed by the restrictions, the supply curve of residential structures would become vertical. If these limits were reached, the asset prices of structures in the community would be higher than they would otherwise have been. Unlike the case of zoning restrictions discussed in the paragraph above, however, there is good reason to believe that communities would institute growth controls during an inflationary period. If price increases were unanticipated, previous residents of the community could experience a reduction in the real value of municipal debt incurred to provide infra-structure—roads, water and sewer systems, schools, etc.—in much the same way that they would have received capital gains from the decline in the real value of mortgages on their houses. Since outstanding debt is repaid by taxes levied on all residents of a community, new residents of a community would, in effect, share part of the gains made by previous residents. It is therefore in the interest of existing residents of a community to limit growth or to impose charges on developers of new residences which compensate them for gains foregone.

Certain other restrictions are also fairly easy to analyze by standard methods. If rent controls hold the rentals of tenant occupied dwellings below the levels that would have been reached in an unregulated market, knowing demand and supply curves for rental accommodation one could easily calculate the effect of such controls on the housing stock. Limitations upon the conversion of rental units to owner-occupied ones would likewise reduce the owner and increase rental stock, with easily determined effects upon the rental values of each kind of housing. It should be emphasized again, however, that the effects are likely to be small if imposed in a single municipality only in a larger urban area, for the relevant stock demand curves are likely to be highly elastic ones. Finally, the impact of forces such as building code restrictions which raise construction costs can be readily assessed by allowing for the shifts in the supply of new construction which they produce.

Most difficult to assess are restrictions which limit the substitution of factors for each other in producing new residential structures. Examples of such restrictions are ones such as large-lot zoning which require builders to use more land per structure than they otherwise would or density restrictions which limit the amount of capital invested per unit of land. To determine the impact of such restrictions one would have to calculate the amounts of factors actually used under the restrictions as compared to input combinations without such restrictions. Doing so would be relatively easy if one knew the production function for structures or for housing services. Alternatively, on the assumption that the production function is homogeneous of degree one in, say, non-land, N, and land, L, one can easily show from a second order Taylor's expansion about the optimal market input levels that

$$Q* = k_N * N^* + k_L * L^* - (k_N k_L / 2\sigma) * (N^* - L^*)^2,$$

where the asterisk means the logarithmic differential or percentage change in the variable so superscripted. Setting Q^* to zero and substituting the L^* implied by minimum lot size restrictions would then yield a quadratic equation whose solution would give the N^* implied by the restriction. Multiplying the percentage input changes by their market prices would then yield the percentage change in construction cost implied by the restrictions. An alternative, and possibly superior, approximation would be the translog approximation to the production function, itself in effect a second order Taylor's expansion in the logs of input and output, with appropriate restrictions for linear homogeneity imposed.

4. RESIDENTIAL FINANCE

Housing is noteworthy for its durability and the fact that it is relatively expensive to acquire piecemeal. For these reasons, finance is especially important insofar as housing markets are concerned. It is not uncommon for someone to pay cash for a refrigerator, a television set or even an automobile. Straight cash purchases of houses are much less common, however. Earlier, the importance of interest rates for the rental value of housing has been described. In this section, I shall concentrate upon the determination of mortgage interest rates and other factors which may have an effect upon the cost of financing the purchase of a house.

Mortgage interest rates are, presumably, established by the interaction of the demand and supply of funds on mortgage markets. The first part of this section will be concerned with the nature of such markets. In recent years, a variety of mortgage instruments other than the traditional fixed-rate, level-payment mortgate have appeared. For this reason I will next explore the determinants of the optimal mortgage contract from both the borrower's and the lender's point of view. I will then consider the question of why these new instruments have developed.

4.1. Mortgage markets

In surveying the literature on residential finance and related topics, one is struck by the lack of theoretical analysis of mortgage markets. There are, to be sure, large numbers of empirical studies of mortgage markets. These, however, are typically guided by little more than assertions that variable Y is influenced by variable X. Due to the dearth of theory specifically developed to explain the behavior of mortgage markets, one must be content with applying general principles to these markets.

When thinking about the demand for mortgage funds, one is struck by the analogy with the demand for productive factors. Funds borrowed on the security of residential real estate are used along with one's own or equity funds to acquire something of value. The latter may be housing, or perhaps something totally different such as a college education for one's child or a boat. To reduce verbage, however, I will neglect possibilities such as the latter in which follows. Viewed in this way, one would expect the demand for mortgage funds to depend both upon the demand for housing and upon the supply of alternative sources of funds.

Consider the problem of a household contemplating the purchase of a house. Equity and borrowed funds are perfect substitutes in production at a price ratio of unity for this purchase. Neither, however, are available at a constant average cost to the household. Equity funds devoted to the house purchase have a progressively greater opportunity cost in terms of foregone purchases of other assets, expenditure on consumption other than housing, or the holding of cash balances. As the quantity of funds borrowed increases, the outstanding balance of the loan at any future time relative to the value of the asset used as security and the earnings and other assets of the borrower grows. Lenders, one supposes, would thus view the loan as riskier and increase the interest rate charged. To minimize the cost of financing the purchase of the asset, the borrower would choose that combination of own and borrowed funds such that the marginal cost per dollar was the same for both soruces, or all sources if borrowing is done from more than one source. The common marginal cost is the marginal cost of capital to the borrower.

As the borrower contemplates the purchases of progressively larger dwellings, there is no particular reason to suppose that he would find the same ratio of equity to borrowed funds optimal. Neither is there any presumption as to how this ratio would change. However, since the marginal cost of all sources of funds would appear to rise, it is clear that the marginal cost of capital to the borrower would increase with the amount spent for a house. In deciding upon the size of house to purchase, the purchaser would compare the schedule of marginal cost of capital with that of the marginal returns to expenditure on housing. The quantity of borrowed funds demanded would then be determined both by the optimal expenditure and the optimal ratio of equity to borrowed funds at that level of expenditure. Some potential borrowers, of course, might find the marginal returns to house purchase less than the marginal cost of capital at any level of expenditure. They would thus borrow nothing.

With a fall in interest rates the marginal cost of capital to potential home purchasers would fall, presumably. One would thus expect the quantity of mortgage funds demanded to increase. In part this increase would result from some borrowers increasing their expenditure on houses. In part, however, the increase would result from new borrowers entering the market. The latter would be composed of those for whom the marginal cost of capital is higher relative to the returns from owner-occupied housing than for those who would borrow at higher rates. One reason for the higher cost of capital is that borrowers prefer to borrow more relative to their expenditure on a house. The frequent observation that average loan-to-value ratios rise as mortgage rates fall need not result from lender requirements, as is so often supposed. The quantity of mortgage loans demanded would also be affected by changes in the demand for housing or in the supply of equity funds. Such factors are likely to change much more slowly than changes in mortgage rates. One would thus expect a relatively stable demand function for mortgage funds.

Quite different kinds of considerations are important when examining the supply function for mortgage loans. The latter, like the supply function for any commodity, would presumably depend upon the returns to mortgage lending, the returns to other kinds of lending, and the costs of funds to mortgage lenders. Many empirical studies have used deposit inflows into banks and thrift institutions as explantory variables. A moment's reflection, however, suggests the inappropriateness of so doing. Like the input and output of any productive process, deposits and loans or securities are simultaneously affected by the same set of forces. Thus, the supply of mortgage loans and the demand for funds by depository lenders are essentially mirror images of each other. Of course, at various times commercial banks and thrift institutions have been subject to ceilings on the rates they have been permitted to offer on certain classes of deposits. Such institutions, like commercial airlines once subject to minimum fares, however, could increase the services they offered customers in a variety of ways. Deposits ceilings were thus at least partly evaded, and it makes little sense to suppose that deposit inflows were exogenously determined.

It has long been appreciated that supply functions of conventionally considered commodities are homogeneous of degree zero in all prices. Stated differently, the appropriate arguments of supply functions are relative, not absolute, prices. The supply function for mortgage lending possesses a similar property, namely invariance under equal absolute increases in all interest rates. Probably the greatest single factor affecting the level of nominal interest rates is expectations of inflation. Inflation tends to increase the prices of commodities in proportion, but expectations of inflation are added to interest rates. Interest rate differentials, then, are the obvious analogue of relative prices.

Factors which affect the relative attractiveness of mortgage and other kinds of lending would not seem to depend upon the absolute level of interest rates, moreover. Different securities or loans may have different administrative costs, differences in default risk and differences in other characteristics. Mortgage loans, for example, typically do not carry provisions for penalty in case of prepayment.

In a period of falling interest rates, borrowers may in effect "call" mortgage loans by making new loans at lower rates to pay off their old loans. Corporate bonds, however, typically contain provisions which prevent bonds from being called for periods of five to ten years. Differences such as were noted above all affect the differences in yields at which lenders might consider mortgages and other securities equally attractive. The costs of making and servicing mortgage loans, however, would not seem to depend upon the absolute level of interest rates. Much the same is the case in regard to default risk. Differences in call protection have effects which depend upon the expected level of future interest rates in relation to current rates rather than upon the level of current rates. I would therefore expect that the difference in rates at which mortgages and other securities are viewed as equally attractive would be independent of the absolute level of interest rates.

More important, perhaps, is the issue of whether the rates at which, say, mortgages and corporate bonds are viewed as equally attractive would depend upon the relative amounts of the stocks or new issues of such securities. To my knowledge, perhaps the most important consideration is the covariance of the yields of mortgages and other securities. If two different securities have yields which vary inversely over time, then including both in a portfolio would reduce the variability in the portfolio's yield. Mortgages, corporate and government securities, however, have yields which tend to vary quite closely together over time. Savings and Loan Associations and Mutual Savings Banks are entitled to deduct an increasing fraction of their earnings up to a maximum from income for federal tax purposes as the fraction of mortgages and related securities in their portfolios increases. Commercial banks and other mortgage lenders, however, receive no such benefits. I would conclude from these considerations that some lenders, at least, would view mortgages and other securities as perfect substitutes at absolute yield differences that compensate them for differences in administrative costs, default risk, and similar characteristics.

Many have asserted that mortgage markets are segmented from other long term security markets and local in character. Others appear to believe that such was the case until about 1970, when mortgage-backed securities began to be developed. This is probably the case because Savings and Loan Associations and, to a lesser extent, Mutual Savings Banks have specialized in mortgage lending. Moreover, since 1962 they have received substantial tax benefits by concentrating upon mortgage lending. Such institutions, however, have made only about half the mortgage loans originated in this country. Commercial banks and, until the 1960's at least, life insurance companies have made large amounts of mortgage loans as well. So long as such institutions make mortgage loans in significant amounts, then mortgage markets are neither segmented from other securities markets nor local. For, surely commercial banks hold a wide range of securities and loans, many of which are acquired in national markets. So long as some lenders, such as commercial banks, view mortgages and other securities as perfect substitutes at an appropriate yield differential, then the relative supply of mortgage loans is perfectly elastic, rather than perfectly inelastic as segmentation would imply.

Another common belief about the mortgage market is that it is chronically in disequilibrium. In particular, it is asserted that the actual mortgage rate is typically below the market equilibrium rate. Thus, it is believed the "availability" of funds, by which is presumably meant the position of the supply schedule, exerts an important effect upon the cost of financing a house purchase. It is difficult to understand how such beliefs originated, and I know of no compelling evidence that the mortgage market so behaves. Indeed, if the relative supply of mortgage loans is highly elastic, as I have suggested above it is, then the notion of an excess demand for mortgage funds at current interest rates is almost meaningless. The only issue of genuine interest is the length of time it takes for the mortgage market to reach equilibrium if displaced.

4.2. Mortgage instruments

Prior to the 1930's mortgage loans in the U.S. were usually what would now be called a five-year balloon mortgage. By this is meant that the loans were made for a five-year period, at the end of which the whole of the principal became due. It was expected both by the borrower and lender that the loan would be renewed at maturity, though at a new prevailing rate of interest. During the banking crisis of the early 1930's, however, many such loans were not renewed, and many borrowers lost their homes. The wave of home foreclosures was widely thought to have contributed to the difficulties of the great depression, and a new kind of mortgage instrument was introduced by the Federal Housing Administration (FHA) in an attempt to prevent the recurrence of earlier difficulties.

The FHA mortgage loan, unlike its predecessors, was fully amortized. The borrower made a level, that is constant over time, payment which covered both principal repayment and interest. Moreover, the contract interest rate of the loan was fixed for a relatively long period. Later, Veteran's Administration (VA) and conventional (not FHA or VA) loans made following World War II were of the same form. With the worsening of inflation in the 1970's and the constant increase in nominal interest rate, however, real mortgage payments rose sharply in the earlier years of a level payment loan. In consequence, some loans were made with gradually increasing nominal payment schedules during the earlier years of the loan. The sharp increase in nominal interest rates in the earlier 1980's and the accompanying difficulties of Savings and Loan Associations led to increased use of loans whose interest rates were adjusted periodicially by some agreed upon formula.

The facts that the nature of mortgage loans has varied over time in this country and has differed as between the U.S. and other countries suggests its form is subject to determination by economic forces. From the borrower's point of view, repayment of a mortgage loan is saving. Consequently, the determination of the optimal time pattern of a mortgage payment is related to the problem of the optimal pattern of consumption over time. Lenders might be thought of as attempting to match the flow of payments from the assets they own with those due on their liabilities. Alternatively, lenders might try to earn an income by maturity intermediation—taking advantage of interest rate differentials as between maturities of different lengths.

The problem of optimizing the flow of consumption over time is so well known as not to require restatement here, were it not for special features of mortgage loans. Two of these lead to interesting modifications of the general problem. One, closely related to the question of moving costs discussed in Section 2, is that mortgage loans are usually extinguished when a house is sold. It thus seems reasonable to assume that the household lives in a given house during the period covered by the optimization. The other is that mortgage loans typically are made for some amount less than the value of the house. Therefore, a constraint that the household may not be in debt for more than some fraction of its assets would also seem appropriate. Requiring that the level of housing consumption be fixed, except perhaps for depreciation, poses no real difficulties in studying the household's optimization problem. The requirement that its assets exceed its debts by some amount, however, renders analytic treatment difficult. The problem is easily solved numerically for a given utility function, though, so it is convenient to formulate it in terms of discrete time periods.

$$\max \sum_{t=1}^{T} U(x_t, q))/(1 + \delta)^{t-1}$$

$$\text{s.t.} \sum_{i=1}^{t} (1+\rho)^{t-i}(y_i - x_i - \rho q) > = 0, \qquad 1 \le t \le T,$$

with equality holding for period T, on the simplifying assumption that the household has no accumulated wealth at the end of its occupancy. In the above, x_t is the consumption of all other commodities in period t, q is consumption of housing (assuming no depreciation, for further simplicity), y_t is income in year t, ρ is the rate of interest and δ the rate of time preference (compare the continuous formulation in Wheaton [16]). The constraint for period t reflects the fact that the household's consumption cannot exceed its income in that period plus its savings accumulated at interest. The necessary conditions for equilibrium are the following:

$$Ux_t = Ux_{t+1}(1 + \rho)/(1 + \delta) + \lambda_t(1 + \delta)^{t-1}$$

$$\sum_{t=1}^{T} U_q(t)/(1 + \delta)^{t-1} = \rho \sum_{t=1}^{T} Ux_t/(1 + \delta)^{t-1}$$

Here, λ_t is the undetermined multiplier associated with the debt constraint for period t. As is so often done for tractability, let $U = a \ln x + b \ln q$. One can then show that if $\lambda_t > 0$ at $t = t_1 - 1$ (or $t_1 = 1$) and $t = t_2$ and $\lambda_t = 0$ for the interval $t_1 - 1 < t < t_2$, then

$$x_{t_1} = \sum_{t=t_1}^{t_2} (y_t - \rho q)/(1 + \rho)^{t-t_1} \bigg/ \sum_{t=t_1}^{t_2} 1/(1 + \delta)^{t-t_1}$$

$$x_t = x_{t_1}[(1 + \rho)/(1 + \delta)]^{t-t_1}$$

Also,

$$q \sum_{t=1}^{T} 1/x_t(1 + \delta)^{t-1} = (b/a\rho) \sum_{t=1}^{T} 1/(1 + \delta)^{t-1}$$

Numerical solutions of the above set of equations yield results that accord with one's intuition. Provided that the rate of interest is small enough as compared with the rate of time preference or discount, the debt constraint becomes binding. The optimal mortgage payment, which consists of saving and housing expenditure, is constant over time. However, at sufficiently higher interest rates the household desires to shift enough consumption from present to future so that the asset constraint no longer is binding. The optimal mortgage payment then tends to increase over time during the initial life of the loan. Given the rate of time preference, the interest rate at which the debt constraint ceases to bind increases with the growth rate of income. Another point worth noting is that in solutions I have calculated housing consumption is affected very little by the debt constraint. This is the case because housing consumption is held fixed throughout the period over which consumption is optimized.

To my knowledge there has been little or no theoretical study of the optimal form of a mortgage loan from the lender's point of view. It is tempting to suppose that lenders prefer a time pattern of payments that matches that of their liabilities. Though life insurance companies and pension funds are lenders that fit this description, until recently the majority of residential first mortgage loans were held by depository lenders. The latter, consisting of commercial banks in addition to thrifts, raise funds for mortgage lending on short-term markets. Historically, depository institutions have profited from so-called maturity intermediation because long-term interest rates have typically exceeded short-term ones. Savings and Loan Associations experienced financial difficulties in the early 1980's, however, when short-term interest rates rose relative to long-term rates.

It is worthy of note that nominal interest rates were relatively low as compared with the rate of inflation during the 1950's and early 1960's. The growth rate of income was relatively high at that time. Consequently, as the analysis above suggests, a level of payment loan may well have been optimal for the consumer. Moreover, there was relatively little fluctuation in interest rates, and long-term interest rates were typically greater than short-term rates. Under such conditions it was relatively profitable for depository lenders to borrow short and lend long. Conditions changed drastically beginning with the late 1960's. A variety of alternative mortgage instruments have since been discussed and experimented with. In recent years the adjustable rate mortgage has made up from one-third to two-thirds of mortgage loans made in the U.S. Under the latter, rates are varied at intervals as short as one year. Such loans are being made available at rates of two or more percentage points below those of fixed rate mortgages. Moreover, depository lenders are selling off fixed rate mortgage loans they make in secondary markets to a great extent. Nominal interest rates which are high relative to the current rate of inflation and highly variable by historical standards appear to have reduced the willingness of depository lenders to bear the risk of interest rate fluctuations.

5. FURTHER ISSUES

To this point the discussion has largely neglected two features which many believe are of crucial importance in the study of housing. These are the durability and heterogeneity of dwelling units. If one views the role of theory as the development of substantive propositions for prediction of real world phenomena rather than literal description, then such omissions may not be of very great importance. However, one can never know how useful it would be for prediction to take features such as durability and heterogeneity seriously until they have been incorporated into formal analysis and their implications developed. Therefore, in this section I shall attempt to do just this, first taking up the implications of durability and then heterogeneity.

5.1. Durability

There are a variety of issues for which questions of durability are important. I have already discussed the implications for housing demand of the fact that households remain in a given dwelling for a period of time rather than moving whenever income, price or other changes occur in Section 2, above. Possibly the most interesting implications of durability are those involving the allocation of a given set of households defined by income and tastes for housing vs. other commodities to a given stock of housing inherited from the past. Such a stock, consisting of dwellings of different size or capacity to satisfy wants, might well not be the optimal distribution given the distribution of households by income and tastes. Durability is of interest for the production of new units of stock since not only present but also future conditions of demand and cost influence the producer's decision of size of units to build. Closely related is the matter of filtering or the succession of occupancy of given dwellings over time as the number and distribution of households change over time. In what follows I will discuss each of these last three issues in turn.

When a given stock of dwellings exists, it may not be possible for everyone to occupy a unit which is in some sense optimal. Rather, the market rental for dwellings of different sizes may have to adjust so as to make a given set of households willing to occupy the existing units. For any given distribution of dwellings by rental value to be an equilibrium one, all households with the same income and tastes for housing vs. other commodities must be at the same level of utility. Thus, as a first step, the maximization of $U = U(x, q)$ subject to $x + R(q) = y$, where $R(q)$ is the market rental as a function of size of dwelling, requires

$$dU = -U_x \, dR + U_q \, dq = 0 \quad \text{or} \quad \partial R / \partial q = U_q / U_x.$$

Integrating the latter gives what has come to be called the bid-rent or rent-offer curve. It's slope is nothing but the marginal rate of substitution of housing, q, for other consumption, x. So long as indifference curves are downward sloping, the bid-rent curve obtained from it by translation and a 180 degree rotation is concave downward.

The market relation between rents and dwelling sizes depends, in addition, upon the distribution of households by income and tastes and the relation of bid-rent curves to these two characteristics. In a housing market equilibrium, higher income households must be on a higher indifference curve. Consequently, so long as housing is a superior good, the slope of the bid-rent curve must be numerically greater for any given size dwelling the higher is the household's income. The situation is similar as regards differences in tastes. One household has stronger tastes for housing than another of the same income if in the same market its consumption of housing is greater. The latter will be the case only if, at a given quantity of housing services, the indifference curve of the former household is steeper than that of the latter.

In addition to the requirement that households with the same income and tastes achieve the same level of utility, a housing market equilibrium requires that any household offer at least as much for the dwelling it occupies as any other household would. As was just indicated, the rent offers of higher income households and those with stronger tastes for housing are relatively higher for larger dwellings. They will thus occupy bigger units in an equilibrium. The market relation of rent to size is the envelope of the bid-rent curves of all groups as defined by income and tastes. The latter groups must be properly arrayed, of course, in accordance with the slopes of their bid-rent curves. The market relationship of rent to size thus not only reflects the fact that households of a given group will offer more for larger dwellings but also the fact that those who value larger dwellings more highly will tend to occupy them.

The absolute level of rent offers depends upon the utility level reached by the households of different groups. This utility level, in turn, depends upon the group's income and the slope of a price line tangent to the indifference curve reached. An increase in this utility level for a given level of money income is associated with a fall in the tangency price and *vice versa*. Moreover, the slope of the bid-rent curve changes as the utility level a given group achieves changes. Since a fall in tengency price is accompanied by a movement to a higher utility level if money income is fixed, the slope of the bid-rent curve becomes steeper for any given quantity of housing. The slope of the bid-rent curve remains unchanged, of course, where utility level is held fixed.

Consider, now, the allocation of a group of households, whose incomes and tastes for housing may differ, to an equal number of dwellings inherited from the past, which differ in size. Tentatively, let the tangency price for each group of households be the same, and order the households from smallest to largest in terms of the slopes of their bid-rent curves. Then, the number of dwelling units available to each of the groups is the number for which its bid-rent curve lies above those of adjacent groups in the ordering. If the number of units available to a particular group exceeds the number of households in that group, then its bid-rent curve and tangency price must fall and the utility level it achieves must rise. Conversely, if the number of available units is less than the number of households, bid-rent and tangency price must rise and its utility level fall. In such a manner, the unit prices paid for housing by different groups of households is determined by a matching households to dwellings in a very short-run housing market equilibrium.

Given such a framework, it is relatively easy to study the immediate effects of changes in the housing stock. Suppose, for example, that a particular governmental program demolishes some privately owned dwelling units and rehouses an equal number of households in newly built units. The consequences for the pattern of private market prices depends upon the relation of the size of dwelling demolished to the size occupied by re-housed households. If those demolished are smaller on the average, then an excess demand for dwellings will exist in the smaller size range. Rent offers of households occupying dwellings of this size must rise. Conversely, market rents would tend to fall in the range of dwelling sizes formerly occupied by re-housed households. Given the bid-rent function, perhaps from some specific form of utility function, together with numerical information on the distributions of households and dwellings, the market rent as a function of size is readily calculated. (For an example of a calculation using groups of discrete size, see Muth [8]. Rosen [13] discusses the nature of the solution for a continuous distribution of sizes demanded.)

Over periods of time sufficiently long for new units to be built, the rentals received by the owners of different sized dwellings must be just sufficient to cover the costs of units of a size being built. The decision problem of the firm providing housing services becomes a more difficult one when the structures providing these services are durable ones. Let $V(t)$ be the value of a dwelling built at time t, $R_t(u)$ the rental expected at time u for the dwelling built at time t, and ρ the rate at which future receipts are discounted. Also let N_t be the amount of non-land factors used in constructing the dwelling, n_t be their unit price at time t, L_t be the amount of land used, and

$r(u)$ be rental value per unit of land expected at time u. Then,

$$V(t) = \int_t^{t+T} R_t(u)\exp[-\rho(u-t)]\,du - n_t N_t$$

$$- L_t \int_t^{t+T} r(u)\exp[-\rho(u-t)]\,du + \exp[-\rho(t+T)]V(t+T).$$

The developer's problem is to select N_t, l_t, and T so as to maximize $V(t)$.

Suppose that competition among developers is sufficiently strong so that at any time the maximum attainable value from new construction is zero. The necessary conditions for an equilibrium then become

$$\int_t^{t+T} (\partial R_t(u)/\partial N_t)\exp[-\rho(u-t)]\,du = n_t$$

$$\int_t^{t+T} (\partial R_t(u)/\partial L_t)\exp[-\rho(u-t)]\,du = \int_t^{t+T} r(u)\exp[-\rho(u-t)]\,du$$

$$R_t(t+T) = L_t r(t+T)$$

The first two conditions are quite similar to the standard ones and relatively easy to interpret. They simply state that the expected discounted marginal value product of a factor over the life of the structure be equal to its unit price. By assumption all expenditures on non-land factors are made at the time of construction, so the appropriate price variable is that of such factors at time t. For land, however, site value is an opportunity cost throughout the structure's life. The appropriate price variable for land is thus its expected discounted rental value. The latter, of course, is equal to its sales price. The third condition relates to the optimal time for replacement of the structure. On the assumption that V is zero at all times t, postponement of redevelopment implies no foregone interest cost on the value of the replacement structure. The developer thus replaces the structure when its rental value has fallen to the rental value of the site upon which it is built.

The assumption that competition among developers eliminates any value from development means, of course, that the expected discounted rental value of the structure over its lifetime equals its cost. The latter is expenditure on construction plus the expected discounted sum of land rentals, or land value. This last condition is closely related to another which is important in analyzing durability. This is that the expected value of development of a site be independent of the time when the site is developed. For otherwise, by delaying or advancing their time of planned development, developers could increase their expected returns. It is presumably for this reason that some sites remain vacant within the built-up area of a city for a time.

As in other areas of economic theory, the matter of what kind of expectations are held by developers is of considerable importance. Some writers (notably Anas [1]) have assumed that expectations are myopic. Others (especially Fujita [3] and Wheaton [17]) have assumed that developers have perfect foresight. What is most important, perhaps, for investment in real estate is the long term growth rate of population, income and construction costs. Certainly, no reasonable developer would suppose these to be zero. At the same time, few if any, for example, would have foreseen the shifts in population from relatively high to low income groups that took place within many parts of U.S. cities during the post World War II period.

To date, the progress made in analyzing models of durable structures has been disappointing at best. Little beyond very general conclusions have been reached unless specific assumptions are made about the mathematical form of utility and/or production functions. Even then, such models are most easily analyzed numerically. Durability has been studied most extensively in models of urban spatial structure, which are discussed elsewhere by Fujita. In this context their principal results seem to be that, unlike the implications of static models, urban residential densities can increase with distance from the center of a city and development can proceed from outside in toward the center. It is by no means clear that such findings contribute very much to our understanding of real world phenomena.

When the production of new housing becomes possible, the problem of allocating households to dwellings discussed earlier becomes rather different. So long as dwellings of a given size are being built, their rentals are presumably fixed by the costs of new units. Thus, rather than rentals it is the size of distribution of newly built dwelling units that adjusts to mismatches in the distribution of dwellings inherited from the past with distribution of households by income and tastes for housing. In the case of the hypothetical governmental program discussed earlier, the combination of demolitions and public construction would have no effect upon dwelling rentals so long as new construction is taking place. Rather, more dwellings than otherwise would be privately built in the size range where demolitions are concentrated and fewer in the ranges where public construction is concentrated. Only if no new construction is taking place within a given size range would rentals shift to bring about adjustment.

The notion of filtering is one of the oldest in the literature on real estate and urban economics. In the earliest, most naive discussions it was simply assumed that new dwelling units would be built for the highest income groups. As dwellings aged it was supposed that they were passed down to lower income groups rather like clothing from older to younger children in large families. A little consideration of the way U.S. cities have developed suggests, however, that such is rarely the case. There are many instances of neighborhoods in U.S. cities which have retained the same relative income class of inhabitants for a half century or more. Since World War II, moreover, there were many instances of sudden shifts in the ethnic character and/or relative income level of neighborhoods. In recent years, many instances of so called gentrification or filtering up have occurred. Calculations made from U.S. Census data suggest that, while new housing tends to have a higher average rental value than existing housing, it tends to be constructed throughout the distribution of dwellings by size.

While I know of relative few analyses, I would expect the pattern of filtering to depend first and foremost upon the relative costs of providing dwelling units of different sizes. If, for example, it is relatively cheaper to build larger units, as some empirical evidence suggests, then relatively more new dwellings will be of above average size, and conversely. Likewise, I would expect that the greater the growth rate of income, and thus of the quantity of housing demanded per household, the greater would be the tendency for upper income households to live in newer dwellings. However, the greater the rate of increase in relative construction costs over time the slower would be the increase in the quantity of housing demanded per household. Construction cost increases, then, would tend to limit the tendency for newly built units to be in the upper end of the range of dwellings by size.

5.2. Multiple attributes

To this point I have treated the commodity we call housing as if it were capable of being described as a scalar magnitude. In recent years there has been considerable objection voiced to this traditional procedure. Real world dwelling units are most certainly characterizable as heterogenous, as anyone who has recently searched for another dwelling will realize. Different units differ in a variety of dimensions, such as square feet of floor space, front footage of lot, quality of construction and condition—to name but a few of the more important ones. Moreover, since they are fixed in location, units differ in terms of their surroundings, the kind of community in which they are located, and their nearness to employment and shopping places. While it is commonplace to think of commodities such as food and clothing in addition to housing, most people assemble their own collections of commodities of these types at grocery and clothing stores. Housing, however, comes pre-bundled, as food would if one were to select from a variety of pre-assembled market baskets at the supermarket.

Considered more carefully, however, many other commodities can be as easily described as a bundle of characteristics. Wine, for example, is a combination of color, bouquet, acid and several other features which can distinguish one year's output of a particular winery from some other. Automobiles are combinations of kind of engine, transmission and sound-system, the presence or absence or features such as air conditioning, and—perhaps most important these days—gas mileage. Indeed, it was to automobiles that the notion of bundle of characteristics was first applied empirically. Nor is the question of multiple attributes unique to commodities, for jobs can be similarly characterized. To some, perhaps, a college professor is a college professor, but to those of us who work at it professorships differ by type of institution, department, teaching load and in many other respects in addition to salary. Housing is thus far from alone in being describable as consisting of a variety of characteristics.

There are several bases for treating a commodity which is seemingly more properly described as a vector of characteristics as if it were a scalar magnitude. One which is quite common, though often unarticulated, is based on the fact that notions such as commodity are artificial constructs used for purposes of theoretical analysis, not for taxonomy. The identification of such constructs with real world entities depends upon the purpose at hand. If results are sufficiently good when, say, treating housing as a scalar magnitude, then the additional complexity of treating it as a vector would seem unjustified. Hopefully, though, theory should provide some insight as to the conditions under which treating an aggregate as if it were a single entity would prove workable.

One of the simplest and most widely applicable rationales for treating housing as a scalar is that based upon some common composite commodity theorem. It has long been known that if the relative prices of a group of commodities are fixed, then that group behaves as if it were a single commodity. In the case of what we call housing, square feet of floor space and number of bathrooms are not really distinct in terms of market magnitudes so long as their relative prices are fixed. The characteristics of the housing bundle are constructed out of materials of various kinds by labor of various skills on a particular piece of land. So long as the relative prices of these inputs are the same, the relative costs of increments to the different characteristics of the housing bundle would remain unchanged.

Perhaps over time but certainly within different parts of an urban area at a given time, the relative prices of some factors are likely to differ, however. It seems highly probable that at a given moment unit prices of construction materials and labor are more or less the same throughout an urban area. Land prices differ strikingly, though, as evidenced by the variation of building heights. While variation in land prices would have but little impact upon the additional cost of another bathroom, the effect upon the cost of yard space would be considerably greater. In such instances it seems reasonable to apply the composite commodity theorem to non-land factors and treat housing as a particular aggregate produced by non-land factors and by land. Other aggregations of productive factors, of course, might be appropriate for the pattern of factor price differences existing in other circumstances.

Still another rationale for treating housing as a single aggregate is based upon the nature of the consumer's utility function. Let the consumer be concerned with characteristics z_i, $i = 1, \ldots, m$, and let these characteristics be functions $z_i = z_i(x_{11}, \ldots, x_{ni})$ of goods x_j which are purchased on the market. The utility function of the household may then be written as

$$U = U(z_1(x_{1i}, \ldots, x_{n1}), \ldots, z_m(x_{1m}, \ldots, x_{nm}))$$

It is then possible to define characteristics and their unit prices as weighted averages of the goods used in their production and the market prices of these goods, respectively. The demand functions for these characteristics depend only upon real income and the prices of all characteritics. The weights of goods and their prices depend upon income elasticities of demand for these goods as well as upon relative expenditure upon them (Muth [10]).

A natural interpretation of the functions z_i is that they describe production taking place within the household. On this interpretation it is reasonable to assume that the z_i are homogenous of degree one in all the goods relevant to their production. The income elasticities of all goods used to produce a given characteristic are then the same. The weights of goods and their prices in determining the values of characteristics and their prices are simply expenditure shares. Moreover, the prices of these characteristics are independent of their quantities and behave in other respects like the prices of conventionally defined commodities (Muellbauer [6]). Muellbaur also notes that the latter properties are also true under homogeneity of the functions z_i and homothetic preferences even if production is joint. I find the latter hypothesis to be rather unappealing, however.

The above, purely formal, results may be interpreted in different ways. On the one hand, characteristics may be thought of as including square feet of floor space and number of rooms. Alternatively, characteristics might be thought to include housing, while floor space and number of rooms might be considered to be goods. Indeed, Murray [7] had demonstrated that the same conditions noted in the paragraph above which are sufficient to insure that the prices of characteristics are independent of their quantity also suffice to permit the definition of a composite commodity called housing services. As Murray notes, however, there are conditions such as fixed relative prices that permit the latter but do not insure that the prices of characteristics are independent of their amounts.

The interest in housing as a bundle of characteristics and the statistical estimation of hedonic price indexes have been mutually reinforcing. An hedonic index for housing is simply a function relating the market rental or value of a dwelling to the various characteristics of the unit itself and to the nature of its surroundings. There can be little doubt that such functions are exceptionally valuable in empirical work. There is considerable variability in real world dwelling units. The variation in such characteristics as square feet of floor space and quality of construction are often so large as to swamp the effects of location, local taxation and expenditure and other characteristics which an investigator might be examining. Moreover, hedonic indexes have proved useful in estimating time and place effects upon housing prices and can be used for a variety of other purposes.

Theory, however, has given little guidance to the appropriate functional form for hedonic indexes. Letting $U = U(z_1, \ldots, z_m, x)$, where x is dollars of expenditure on everything other than housing characteristics z_i, the necessary conditions for maximizing U subject to $x + R(z_1, \ldots, z_m) = y$ are $U_i/U_x = R_i$, $i = 1, \ldots, m$. Substituting these, the household's bid-rent function may be written as

$$dR = \sum_{i=1}^{m} (U_i/U_x)\, dz_i$$

This development suggests that the coefficients of a characteristic in explaining rent offers would vary inversely with the amounts of the characteristic relative to all other consumption. However, where $U = U(q(z_1, \ldots, z_m), x)$ the ratio U_i/U_j depends upon the relative marginal productivity of the two characteristics. The differential in rental may then be written as

$$dR = (U_q/U_x)\sum_{i=1}^{m} q_i\, dz_i$$

On the interpretation that q is a production function for housing services, q_i depends upon the relative amounts of the different characteristics used in production. The term U_q/U_x, however, indicates that the coefficients of the bid-rent function still depend upon the amount of housing relative to other commodities.

Many empirical studies have taken the estimated coefficients of hedonic price indexes and used them as price variables in further statistical analysis. Like the market bid-rent function, however, the market hedonic price function is an envelope of the individual household bid-rent functions. Several authors (specifically, Brown and Rosen [2]) have pointed out that such second stage analyses may contain no information which is additional to that provided by the estimated hedonic function itself. Though the problem has by no means been fully explored, intuitively the hedonic coefficients are functions of variables such as income and tastes which lead different households to consume different bundles of characteristics. If these same variables are used to explain variations in the demand for characteristics, the demand equations presumed to do so may not be identified.

References

[1] Anas, A. (1978) Dynamics of urban residential growth. *Journal of Urban Economics*, **5, 66–78
[2] Brown, J. N. and Rosen, H. S. (1982) On the estimation of structural hedonic price models. *Econometrica*, **50, 765–68.
*[3] Fujita, M. (1982) Spatial patterns of residential development. *Journal of Urban Economics*, **12**, 22–52.
**[4] Marshall, A. (1950) *Principles of Economics*, 8th edn. New York: The Macmillan Co.
*[5] McFadden, D. (1976) Qualitative choice analysis. *Annals of Economic and Social Measurement*, **5**, 363–90.
[6] Muellbauer, J. (1974) Household production theory, quality, and the 'hedonic technique'. *American Economic Review*, **64, 977–94.
*[7] Murray, M. (1978) Hedonic prices and composite commodities. *Journal of Urban Economics*, **5**, 188–97.
*[8] Muth, R. F. (1978) The allocation of households to dwellings. *Journal of the Regional Science Association*, **18**, 159–78.
*[9] Muth, R. F. (1973) Capital and current expenditures in the production of housing. In *Government Spending and Land Values*, edited by C. Lowell Harris, pp. 65–78. Madison, Wis.: The University of Wisconsin Press.
[10] Muth, R. F. (1966) Household production and consumer demand functions. *Econometrica*, **34, 699–708.
*[11] Muth, R. F. (1974) Moving costs and housing expenditure. *Journal of Urban Economics*, **1**, 108–25.
*[12] Reid, M. G. (1962) *Housing and Income*. Chicago: The University of Chicago Press.
*[13] Rosen, S. (1974) Hedonic prices and implicit markets: production differentiation in pure competition. *Journal of Political Economy*, **82**, 34–55.
[14] Siegan, B. H. (1970) Non-zoning in Houston. *Journal of Law and Economics*, **13, 71–147.

**[15] Smith, L. B. *et al.* (1982) The demand for housing, household headship rates, and household formation. Working paper 82–55, Center for Real Estate and Urban Economics, UC Berkeley.

*[16] Wheaton, W. C. (1985) Life-cycle theory, inflation and the demand for housing. *Journal of Urban Economics,* **18,** 161–79.

*[17] Wheaton, W. C. (1982) Urban residential growth under perfect foresight. *Journal of Urban Economics,* **12,** 1–21.

Topics in Empirical Urban Housing Research

ALLEN C. GOODMAN

Department of Economics, Wayne State University, USA.

1. INTRODUCTION

The urban housing researcher of policy analyst is faced with a substantial gap between the illuminating, but perhaps overly simple, theoretical models, and the analytical problems which occur in the empirical examination of housing market processes. Urban economics presents a well-developed body of theory that determines land rents and population densities in terms of the journey-to-work, the locations of the rich and the poor and the construction (and/or demolition) of the urban housing stock. Housing analysis has developed in this context with good specification of supply, demand and market equilibrium for an urban area that is dominated by a central place.[1]

However, the housing theory is much less helpful in providing guidance for the measurement of behavioral parameters. In the "real world," housing is purchased jointly with both neighborhood and local public goods. Substantial moving and transactions costs for both buyers and sellers impede the costless adjustment to changed prices, costs, or incomes that generally characterize the modeling of demand and supply. Data inadequacies may further complicate the analysis with econometric problems that require special treatment.

The past twenty-five years has seen an explosion of micro-economic and micro-econometric research on urban housing. Since the location of households in an urban area has been one of the primary foci of modern urban economic analysis, characterization of the residential housing decision has been important to urban economic theory. As a result, the conceptualization and measure-

---

[1] The *monocentric* model is discussed in more detail in Section 2.

ment of demand, supply and market equilibrium have had substantive impacts, not only in the derivation of urban location and housing theory, but also in the formulation of housing policies at both the national and local levels.

This discussion suggests three fundamental aspects of empirical housing market analysis. First, housing markets are largely defined within urban areas. Second, housing markets have several features that distinguish them from other types of markets. Third, housing market analyses, even in their most basic forms, are fundamentally important in more general urban and policy analyses.

The emphasis on the *urban* nature of the housing markets is dictated by more than the simple assertion that housing is an urban problem because 70 percent or more of the households live in urban areas. Rather, it must address many spatially related aspects of the housing market that are most salient (and, in fact, are generally defined only) within urban areas. The bundling of the housing purchase with neighborhood or with location relative to workplace, for example, is an urban problem. Rental (as opposed to owner-occupied) housing is disproportionately located in urban areas (most particularly, central cities). This has major urban spatial implications, with households reacting to policies (such as tax policies) that may favor the purchase of owner (suburban) rather than rental (central city) units.

The empirical examination of urban housing markets must also consider several features that differentiate urban housing markets from other types of markets. It will become apparent that these features are neither exhaustive, nor necessarily mutually exclusive. They do suggest, however, several analytical concerns that must be addressed in both theoretical and empirical work:

1) Within a given year, over 90 percent (and in many locations, close to 100 percent) of urban housing services come from existing units, and a substantial rental market exists side-by-side with the market for owner housing. This has several implications. The high costs of maintaining and changing the housing bundle suggests substantial difficulties in landlords' adjusting supplies of services incrementally.[2]

---

[2] In this monograph, I will refer to the *flow* of housing services from the *stock* that provides these services.

2) High search and transactions costs for both buyers and sellers complicate the usual definitions of either short or long run equilibrium.

3) The housing purchase is inexorably linked to the purchase of other goods, most particularly neighborhood, public services, and workplace accessibility.

4) Perhaps because of these linkages to this large number of bundled components, the housing purchase, and/or adjustment, is quite sensitive to both household and market demographics.

5) For many households, the housing purchase represents not only shelter, but also the largest (and often only) source of accumulated savings.

These features suggest important concerns in both the modeling and the analyses that emerge from urban housing studies. Many maintained assumptions from standard economic theory can lead to serious analytical problems if they are applied to the modeling and measurement of housing market behavior.

Moreover, both the theoretical and empirical housing market analyses have profound and substantive roles in more general urban analysis. The *income elasticity of housing demand* is crucial to the discussion of both urban structure and urban housing policy. In constructing urban economic theory, a primary concern (and early success) of urban modeling was to explain the seeming paradox of the rich living further from downtown, on less expensive land, while the poor live closer in on more expensive land (Alonso, 1964, Mills, 1972, and Muth, 1969). Increased income implies increased demand for housing (land). Due to the lower price and to the availability of land on which to construct the housing, further away from the central place, the increased demand is generally associated with a longer commute to work. The opportunity cost of this commute may also rise with income (or, more properly, wage rate). If the income elasticity of housing, or land, demand is higher (lower) than the income elasticity of commuting costs, increased income leads to increased (decreased) commuting.[3]

---

[3] This is discussed in more detail in Section 2.1, below.

Early aggregate studies of housing demand, such as Reid [1962] or Muth [1960] were quite supportive of this theory, finding large housing income elasticities (which, by inference, were greater than travel time elasticities). More recent household-level studies (summarized in Quigley, 1979, and Mayo, 1981) provide much lower demand elasticity estimates (often +0.5 or lower). If these micro-econometric estimates are valid, then the use of income elasticities to support the locations of the rich and the poor is less persuasive.

Uncertainty as to the income elasticity has also affected *housing policy* analysis. Almost all studies have shown that programs in which the government supplies housing to the poor are very expensive. Cash, or demand side subsidies, would provide a textbook case of improved economic efficiency. Further, from the early (high) estimated income elasticities, it would also lead to large increases in housing demand. Again disaggregated measurements, either from cross-sectional analyses mentioned above, or from the Experimental Housing Assistance Program (see Bradbury and Downs, 1982) presented income and price elasticities far below those that had been accepted as "common knowledge." Although economists might argue that the cash subsidies are still preferable to in-kind aid, policy analysts might resist such programs if they are more concerned about increasing housing consumption by the poor.

It is clear that a thorough examination of all of the empirical aspects of housing market analysis would be far beyond the scope of this monograph. I will consider three topics that are urban in nature, that address the special features of the housing market, and that have implications for urban theory and policy. These topics are loosely defined within the purview of household and/or landlord levels of demand and/or supply, yet have often been "lost in the shuffle" of maintained hypotheses, or "topics to be discussed later."

Neighborhood has been largely ignored in the characterization of housing demand or supply. At least as pervasive a stylized fact as the downward sloping rent gradient within urban areas, is the fact that a city (even with presumably equal public inputs into the production of public services) is a patchwork of individual neighborhoods. These neighborhoods must be purchased with the housing bundle, and are subject to preferences that cannot be explained either by accessibility or by public inputs. Perhaps because neighborhood is difficult to measure, and more difficult to model, economists have often asserted that it does not make much difference. If such is the case, then the observed ethnic and racial enclaves that obviously exist have no economic meaning. Further, this assertion implies that realtors, home buyers, and the general public are misguided or misinformed in their statements that neighborhood is important, and in their perceived willingness to pay premiums for at least some neighborhood amenities. It is thus necessary to examine both the modeling and the empirical concerns of neighborhood as part of the housing purchase.

A second topic involves long term v. short term demand and supply behavior. Many have maintained that demand is best measured among *movers,* who are presumed to be closest to some form of single period equilibrium. This discussion occurs with full knowledge that owners, in particular, move very seldom, that moving costs (even for renters) entail nontrivial transactions costs, and that moving may involve a substantial loss of accumulated consumer surplus in terms of proximity to neighbors and familiarity with local resources (Dynarski, 1981). Similar distinctions between the long and short terms are appropriate with respect to the sale of existing home, and/or to the landlord's decision to change tenants or to leave a unit vacant.

The third topic to be addressed concerns the treatment of demographics in microeconomic and spatial housing market analysis. The monocentric model treats households as containing single workers who work downtown. Multi-worker households may exhibit different commuting patterns and housing demand, and large households presumably consume more housing, but other demographic variables are largely unstudied. It is unclear what happens (as in the 1970s) to either housing demand or household location patterns with a precipitous fall in household size. This section looks at the impacts of urban housing demographics on both the monocentric model and on the measurement of housing demand.

The various sections of the monograph will begin with theoretical foundations, followed by discussions of empirical problems. Econometric problems that are general in scope (such as specification errors or simultaneity biases) will be handled in other mongraphs in this series; those that are more urban in nature will be considered in more detail here. Finally, the availability of fast mainframe and personal computers has led to an enormous improvement in both the analytical capabilities and in the aspirations for improved data. In this context, where applicable, the special features and problems of urban data sets will also be considered.

For a general overview, I refer the reader to several collections of readings, and journals, all of which cover specific topics in detail.[4] These works contain varying proportions of theory and policy, but they provide the detailed discussions of current research. The research presented in this monograph concentrates on the modeling of microeconomic behavior in an urban (spatial) context, in which neighborhoods exist, transportation costs matter, and land rents and housing prices explicitly vary. Other topics, such as the time-series analysis of housing markets, or the examination of housing finance, while obviously urban in context (since over 70 per cent of all housing activity *does* occur in cities), do not necessarily appeal to urban economic analysis in their formulation.

2. NEIGHBORHOOD

This section considers the special problems that involve the treatment of neighborhood effects within an urban housing model. Since much of the urban housing analysis proceeds from the basis of a fairly standard urban location model, it is appropriate to sketch that model, and to discuss its implications. This is followed by a brief discussion of early forms of neighborhood analysis. The measurement of neighborhood effects is then examined, using both hedonic price and discrete choice models, and characterizing both the demand for and the supply of neighborhood characteristics. The final portion considers the implications of neighborhood variables in the analysis of the comparative statics of housing price changes.

---

[4] Miezkowski and Straszheim [1979] is the most recent "classic" set of readings. Bradbury and Downs [1982] sums up much of the recent policy work concerning the EHAP project. Mills [1987] is an excellent collection of recent urban work. Outside of the general economics journals, the specialist should consider the *Journal of Urban Economics, Land Economics, Regional Science and Urban Economics, Urban Studies,* and the *American Real Estate and Urban Economics Journal.*

2.1. The monocentric model

The genesis of urban economics as a separate field, apart from applied microeconomics, may be related to the development of the monocentric model of urban location. This model (Alonso, 1964, Muth, 1969 and Mills, 1972) was derived to explain several general observations about the urban spatial structure:

1) The centralization (and later, *decentralization*) of business and productivity activity relative to residential activity.

2) The high densities, land rents, and housing prices occurring in urban downtown areas, diminishing with distance and/or commuting time.

3) The general tendencies of low (high) income residents to live in high (low) priced housing near (away from) the city's center.

The monocentric model operates on the premise that transportation to the downtown workplace is costly, either in time or in distance. For households to be indifferent among locations, the price of land (and by implication, housing) must change (falling with decreased accessibility) to offset the increased commuting costs. This generates a negative relationship between housing price and distance, or time, to the central place.

Consider a simple model in which the household values a composite consumption good, c, with price 1, and housing services, h, with price $p(u)$ which varies with the travel time u to downtown.[5] Only time costs are considered for commuting; total time T is spent on labor u_l and commuting u.[6] The Lagrange problem, involves maximizing utility function $U(c, h)$ subject to income constraint:

$$y = c + p(u)h$$

and time constraint:

$$T = u_l + u.$$

The corresponding Lagrange optimization is:

$$\mathscr{L} = U(c, h) + \lambda_1(y - c - p(u)h) + \lambda_2(T - u_l - u). \qquad (1)$$

---

[5] Wheaton [1979] shows the formal equivalence between housing and land prices in most monocentric models.

[6] Out-of-pocket costs can be included in the income constraint without changing the analysis.

Optimization over c, h, λ_1, and λ_2 is standard. Optimization with respect to u yields the important first order condition:

$$(\partial p/\partial u)h = -\lambda_2/\lambda_1. \qquad (2)$$

The left hand side, often referred to as the *bid-rent* (or *bid-price*) function, refers to the change in the price of housing, multiplied by the amount of housing; the right hand side is easily interpreted as the negative of the marginal valuation of travel time, $\lambda_2/\lambda_1 = (\partial U/\partial u)/(\partial U/\partial y) = (\partial y/\partial u)$. The housing price gradient must fall with decreasing accessibility to downtown (to offset the rising commuting costs), and flatten as marginal travel costs decrease. The consumer is in equilibrium at the location at which the marginal decrease in housing prices, $(\partial p/\partial u)h$ exactly compensates the increased cost of commuting, $-\lambda_2/\lambda_1$. The decreased prices, as u increases, also lead to increased h.

The impacts of changes in income and commuting costs are then determined by differentiating (2) with respect to y. Defining the marginal valuation of travel time, λ_2/λ_1, as ψ, totally differentiating (2), and substituting $(\partial p/\partial u) = -\psi/h$:

$$du/dy = (\eta_{hy} - \eta_{\psi y})(\psi/y)/(\partial^2 p/\partial u^2). \qquad (3)$$

where η_{hy} is the income elasticity of housing demand, and $\eta_{\psi y}$ is the income elasticity of the valuation of commuting time. Stability requires that $(\partial^2 p/\partial u^2)$ be positive. Hence, if η_{hy} is greater (less) than the $\eta_{\psi y}$, increased incomes lead to longer (shorter) commutes.

There are several ways in which this analysis can be elaborated. If income is divided into *dividend* income and *wage* income (defined as the wage rate, multiplied by u_l), then (3) can be shown to have a pure income effect (interpretable as a change in dividend income, which does not change the marginal valuation of time, hence commuting costs), and a wage effect (which may be positive or negative). If there is no dividend income, and travel time is valued at the wage rate, then $\eta_{\psi y} = 1$, which was first pointed out by Becker [1965]. In this presentation, separate treatment of income and time, with separate constraints, clarifies the interpretation of (2) and the derivation of (3).

This model illustrates housing's substantial impact on the urban structure. Since housing demand determines the locations of residents, and therefore the construction of dwellings, it shapes the structure or the urban area, the uses of land and the demand for transportation. As noted above, the early housing demand literature, with high income elasticities of demand for housing, supported the interpretation of (3) in explaining the decentralization of cities; more recent parameter estimates call this interpretation into question.

The analytical advantage of the monocentric model is its ability to characterize land and/or housing in two dimensions, size and accessibility, and to generate closed-form analytical solutions in its description of spatial equilibrium (see Wheaton, 1979, for a good discussion and summary). The very simple nature of the model, however, renders it less suitable to address more specific problems for housing markets. The introduction of multiple workplaces (and multiple worker households) leads to enormous analytical problems. Many demand and supply aspects of the housing purchase require that one view the dwelling unit as a *bundle* of components, including size and location, but also quality and neighborhood. The substantial transactions costs of mobility (on the part of buyers), and of demolition and preparation (on the part of sellers), also preclude the facile characterization of long run equilibrium required by the monocentric model.[7]

Since the monocentric model considers housing to be completely determined by lot size and accessibility to the central place, it provides little influence for neighboring activities. Consider, instead, a housing parcel as a *bundle* containing two types of components. *Structural* components, S, are privately controlled by the owner or renter. *Neighborhood* components, N, are determined in whole, or in part, by the decisions of others. The two component types probably represent regions of a continuum rather than necessarily exclusive categories. Air-conditioning, bathroom fixtures or roofing material are good examples of structural components. Local public goods, air or water pollution, highway proximity, or types of neighbors, are good examples of the second. Although air pollution (a neighborhood component), for example, might affect roofing material type (a structural component), the forthcoming discussion will treat the two component types as independent.[8]

---

[7] Fujita [1987] discusses many of the useful analyses that can be derived from the monocentric model.

[8] Throughout this monograph, *components* (purchased in the market) will be valued as purchased; they will be distinguished from *characteristics* which are created through a household production function. (Lancaster, 1967). Characteristics will be used below in the discussion of *quasi-public* goods.

2.2. Neighborhood—early analysis

Neighborhood is important due to its spatial linkage to the housing purchase. Since there are limited numbers of both dwelling units and neighborhoods, the linkage may involve some constraint on the otherwise unrestricted tastes for either structural or neighborhood components. Moreover, once settled in a given location, one is subject to the externalities that neighborhood effects impose.

The economics literature provides useful early literature on neighborhoods. Models based on theories of von Thünen and Lösch defined neighborhood by distance, showing how similar activities would gather at similar locations due to market forces, leading to hierarchies of activities both within and among regions. Sociologists (often referred to as the "Chicago School") enhanced the urban context, often by appealing to economic forces. In concentric ring analysis, attributed to Park and Burgess [1925], and interpreted by Guest [1977], higher bids for the centralized locations led to more congestion, causing flight by "higher status" individuals. Different economic or social groups gathered in rings around the central business district, largely in response to impersonal economic market forces.[9] Hoyt [1939] recognized the importance of transportation systems (often radial roads or rail systems) that lead to sectors that can be superimposed on the concentric rings. This, too, implies the clustering of activities into recognizable areas.

The same logic leads to a clustering of activities in the monocentric model as well. In the simplest cases (e.g. the model sketched above), rings and/or sectors defined by income levels evolve, even though income does not enter the consumers' utility functions. Comparative statistics analysis is then used to evaluate the impacts of changes in transportation costs, income, or population size. In contrast to much of the economic analysis, however, the sociologists (and later economic geographers) have been more attentive to the dynamics of the process of change. Their "zone in transition," for example, details the process by which one type of neighborhood (typically of lower social class) expands spatially to take area formerly occupied by a second neighborhood.

Another neighborhood dimension evolved with the recognition and measurement of racial housing segregation (measuring the

---

[9] Guest refers to this as a "nonpersonalistic framework," in contrast to alternative frameworks in which individuals act out of dislike or fear of each other.

separation of groups, typically defined by race) by Taeuber and Taeuber [1965] and followers. Segregation indices comparing racial composition of small areas with overall metropolitan composition indicated concentrations that vary from random distributions. Unlike the economic outcomes above, where concentrations of activities could conveivably be explained by cost conditions or incomes, repeated attempts to explain ethnic or racially-based neighborhoods solely (or even primarily) as the results of *non-personalistic* (to borrow Guest's terminology) market processes determined by income level or housing type, were unsuccessful. Furthermore, many (for example, Kain, 1968) have been able to show that neighborhood racial segregation, itself, may have measurable impacts on the ability of residents to find jobs, and hence on incomes.

Although the difference is apparent to most economists, many other social scientists would find the conceptual gulf between market segregation (the separation of group members *either* by coercion or choice) and market discrimination (difference in economic treatment of group members, which may or may not be manifested in segregation) to be puzzling. Certainly an impetus to the development of urban economics as a separate field in the 1960s was the problem of black-white relationships in urban areas at that time. Pioneering work by Becker [1957] and Bailey [1957] helped to define discriminatory behavior in neighborhoods, and in housing and labor markets, based on racial characteristics. Schelling [1971] provided an ingenious model for looking at dynamic aspects of discriminatory behavior within the housing market. Courant, Yinger and other economists working at Princeton in the early 1970s provided major advances in fitting this type of behavior into the accepted monocentric model. Much of the work, however, concentrated on the *measurement* of neighborhood effects. The adaptation of hedonic price models to housing markets helped to provide a useful framework.

2.3. Measurement

2.3.1. Hedonic price models

The most direct linkages of housing and neighborhood effects can be traced to the development of hedonic price models of housing markets. Popularized by Griliches [1971], these models recognized that goods could be considered as bundles of attributes, or components. Goods that were not explicitly valued in the market, such as clean air, could be valued implicitly by comparing parcels or dwelling units with differing air qualities. Housing demand could be decomposed into the demand for the various components of the housing bundle, including neighborhood.[10]

Following Rosen [1974], let market rent R (alternatively capitalized value) of the dwelling unit be a function of the levels of S and N:

$$R = R(S, N), \qquad (4)$$

where the hedonic price functions, $\partial R / \partial s_i$ and $\partial R / \partial n_i$ represent incremental market valuations of the elements s_i and n_i. Conventional optimization procedures maximize a utility function $U(S, N)$, subject to budget constraint:

$$y = R(S, N) + c \qquad (5)$$

where c, a composite consumption good, is normalized with price 1 (distance and/or time costs that are typically and appropriately included in the monocentric model are ignored here for clarity). First order conditions are standard, with:

$$(\partial U / \partial s_i)/(\partial U / \partial c) = \partial R / \partial s_i, \quad \text{and} \quad (\partial U / \partial n_i)/(\partial U / \partial c) = \partial R / \partial n_i.$$
$$(6)$$

The hedonic prices of elements s_i or n_i, $\partial R / \partial s_i$ and $\partial R / \partial n_i$, represent the joint envelope of suppliers' marginal offer (O_j) curves $(\partial O_j / \partial n_i)$, and demanders' marginal bid (B) curves $(\partial B_j / \partial n_i)$. In Figure 1 (drawn for neighborhood component n_1) the suppliers' marginal offers (shifting due to supply parameters) are upward sloping, consistent with increasing marginal costs; the demanders' marginal bids are downward sloping (shifting due to demand parameters), consistent with decreasing marginal utility. The locus of intersecting marginal offers and bids (at levels n_{1j}) is $\partial R / \partial n_1$, the hedonic price schedule for component n_1.

---

[10] The literature on hedonic prices is voluminous. Rosen [1974] is generally considered to provide the best theoretical discussion; Freeman [1979] presents applications to the measurement of amenity values.

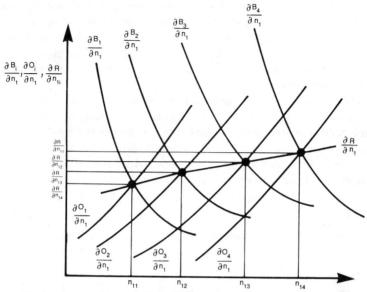

FIGURE 1   Marginal bids, marginal offers and hedonic prices, for a neighborhood attribute.

Rosen notes also that assumptions of linearity (constant marginal valuations) in the underlying hedonic price functions require either constant returns to scale in production, or the costless repackaging of two or more bundles, conditions which cannot reasonably be imposed on most models. The function, then, must be estimated so as to allow nonlinearity in both structural and neighborhood components, and the consensus of empirical studies (e.g. Goodman and Kawai, 1984) is that the functions are nonlinear, leading to well-known problems in demand estimation.[11]

Much of the early measurement of neighborhood effects, including *price-distance* and air pollution functions involved specification of hedonic price equation (4) with vector N, allowing the imputation of values to the vector attributes that do not explicitly enter the market on their own. After some discussion of the desirability of including neighborhood sociodemographic attributes in hedonic price equations (for example Lapham, 1971), most have come to

---

[11] Epple [1987] provides a detailed discussion of estimation pitfalls.

agree that racial, ethnic, and class attributes are also appropriate. This inclusion may lead to some interpretative problems in practice, since neighborhood attributes may be correlated with actual household characteristics (e.g., high income people live in high income neighborhoods), thus confounding the neighborhood price effects with demand effects.[12]

The signs of the neighborhood coefficients have often been either statistically insignificant or wrong. Many analysts have interpreted such findings to mean that, all in all, neighborhood attributes are not important to consumers. Such interpretations suggest that those who object to certain neighborhood attributes choose to live elsewhere; those who remain are indifferent.

Four aspects of the hedonic specification suggest the need for further research:

1) Specification of coefficient structures over space and/or time.

2) Treatment of variable multicollinearity.

3) Spatial autocorrelation of error terms.

4) Proper formulation of null hypotheses about neighborhood effects.

The first three are econometric concerns, and are discussed in some detail in this section. The last involves the more explicit characterization of neighborhood dynamics, and is considered briefly here, and in more detail later in the monograph.

Stability of coefficients is a problem that pervades hedonic studies of all types (including automobiles, housing, and hedonic wage models); price structures are not as stable as one would hope. Replicative estimates from year to year, or from market to market, often differ statistically (by standard tests), with varying signs. Imposing the same coefficients is clearly wrong (tantamount to freezing relative prices in a conventional price index); it is also hard to imagine the implicit prices of such standard bundle components as lot size, living space, number of rooms, distance, or school quality moving from significance to insignificance, or to the wrong sign from year to year, as often occurs.

---

[12] Bartik and Smith [1987] is one of many survey articles.

Second, methods must be developed to determine the proper choice of variables, and to treat the multicollinearity that affects the efficiency of the estimators. Unfortunately, for the estimation of hedonic housing price parameters, many sets of components are not orthogonal. Lot size is often correlated with living space, which is correlated with number of rooms. Among neighborhood components race, income level, education and condition of (neighborhood) housing stock are again often correlated. Although hedonic regressions with groups of multicollinear regressions may have good predictive power, it is very difficult to estimate stable and/or meaningful coefficients of the individual components. Researchers are then forced (often arbitrarily) to omit variables that they would like to include, but which confound the interpretations of the others. In that situation, it then becomes difficult to interpret properly the coefficient of the variable that is estimated.

Component multicollinearity may justify the legitimate and plausible use in economic analysis of either data reduction methods such as *factor analysis* or estimation processes such as *ridge regression*. Factor analysis groups components that vary together, and provides estimated weights for these components in a factor score. One might consider factor analysis as the creation of an index with weights, interpreted as contributions to the factor, being determined by the data. Although it might be noted that the choice of variables in the factor is arbitrary, i.e. determined by the algorithm, this need not be the case. The component vector (which may differ from one determined through the variance minimization procedures of factor analysis) can be specified, and factor weights estimated, and compared to those in the unconstrained model.

This type of specification is compatible with the premise that a household, when buying *neighborhood* does not consider a vector of 20 to 30 neighborhood attributes, but rather looks at attributes such as *schools, crime, shopping* or *neighbors*. These attributes might prove to be very similar to factors created through factor analysis. Economists often criticize factor analysis methods as "data-mining," or as the creation of variables without economic meaning, yet the methods have successfully been used in a number of studies to examine the determination and impacts of neighborhood attributes. For a good discussion of the fundamental econometric aspects of factor analysis, see Dhrymes [1970]. King [1973], Little [1976], and

Dubin and Goodman [1982] use these methods in the measurement of neighborhood components.

Ridge regression (Anderson, 1979) treats the near-singularity of variance-covariance matrices that is brought about through multi-collinearity. In this method, a constant or *ridge* parameter is added to the elements of the variance-covariance matrix. This results in biased coefficients, with reduced standard errors. Problems have been noted with the sensitivity of the estimates to the ridge parameter, which is entirely *ad hoc*. On the other hand, given the typical instability of hedonic coefficients over time and location, the trade-off between econometric bias and econometric efficiency may be worth considering.

Spatial autocorrelation concerns the spatial correlation of the error terms and can take two forms (which may occur jointly). The first involves an omitted common factor among all of the observations. For example, several houses in the same neighborhood might be subject to the same common externality (e.g. zoning regulation); the result is a spatially correlated error structure, which can lead to inefficient estimation of the parameters. The solution to this form of spatial autocorrelation, in principle, is the specification of the proper parameter that is common to all of the observations. If, however, the true neighborhood boundaries are not known, commonly used neighborhood indicators (typically defined over Census tracts or block groups, or over school districts or political boundaries), which do not properly describe the neighborhood, may not solve the problem.

The second form of spatial autocorrelation involves distance from other observations. If one is considering sales prices of houses, for example, positive error terms in the sale of houses at one location may influence the sales prices considerably at nearby locations, and less so at more distant locations. This form of autocorrelation is similar but much more complicated than time series autocorrelation. In the time series case, causality is one-dimensional (time) and unidirectional (past to future). In the spatial case, the appropriate error term can be characterized in at least two spatial dimensions and in multiple directions. Consistent and efficient estimators have been developed by Dubin (1988) for the case in which the error term can be treated as an exponentially decreasing function of distance from the other observations.

The fourth aspect of hedonic specification involves the proper formulation of hypotheses on neighborhood effects. The traditional model has allowed us to assume that preferences are identical. Hence, if a city block is made into an airport (overnight, and totally unexpectedly), then it is assumed that all of the residents will assess the negative benefit of aircraft noise equally, and, in the long term, property values will reflect the proximity to the airport (i.e. noise). Suppose, however, some residents do not mind airport noise, and others who do, can sell to those who do not mind. Then the measured property value discounts will reflect the valuations of the marginal buyer (who, in this case, does not mind the noise very much) when treated in a hedonic price equation.[13]

Further, the traditional models have assumed that neighborhood development occurs independently of other neighborhood development. Suppose, for example, that businesses, who are not overly concerned about the airport noise, bid away the land closest from the airport from residents. One can envision two possible responses to this change in land use. The first is the desire for office workers to live close to the office, leading to increased prices. The second is the reluctance to live so close to high density office space, leading to decreased prices. Again, the price effects may be localized and less predictable than the simple theory might dictate. Strange [1987] presents a novel analysis of this problem, which is discussed in more detail below.

2.3.2. Discrete choice models

Discrete choice (referred to here as multinominal logit, or *MNL*) methods have become popular for measuring neighborhood impacts in the last 10 years (in large part because of improved estimation procedures and computation speed). Following McFadden [1974], these models use, as a point of departure, the self-evident proposition that the residential choice is a discrete one (households live either in one place or another). The bundle that is chosen is compared with bundles that are *not* chosen (all of them together forming a *choice set*), allowing inferences as to the impacts of

---

[13] This result is well known in the analysis of price differentials of financial instruments. Municipal bond prices, for example, reflect the marginal tax rates of those buyers with the *highest* marginal tax rates.

attributes that vary among the bundles. This section reviews some of these models briefly, looking first at the analysis following McFadden, and then at an alternative formulation provided by Ellickson [1981].

Specification of the appropriate *MNL* choice sets has been a problem, since cities have hundreds of thousands of dwelling units available, within hundreds of neighborhoods. With the least sophisticated *MNL* analysis, this would lead to hundreds or thousands of choices in the simplest of problems. As a result, much of the analysis has been arbitrary in choice of dwelling unit or location. In addition, several problems with the maintained hypothesis of the independence of irrelevant alternatives (often termed *IIA,* and requiring that the odds of picking alternative *i* relative to alternative *j* be independent of the characteristics of all other available alternatives) led to major concerns about the applicability of the method.[14]

More recent versions of the model, usually referred to as *nested multinomial logit,* or *NMNL,* allow the partitioning of choices into a hierarchy of choices, providing both more tractable estimation procedures of the models, and more intuitively pleasing treatments of the neighborhood choice. In particular, they allow the relaxing of the *IIA* requirement. As in the hedonic price discussion, partition the bundle of services jointly into two types of components, structural and neighborhood.[15] The probability of choosing dwelling unit *j* and neighborhood *i* is:

$$\phi(i, j) = e^{\alpha_1 N_{1i} + \alpha_2 S_{2j}} \Big/ \sum_{m=1}^{C} \sum_{n=1}^{N_m} e^{\alpha_1 N_{1m} + \alpha_2 S_{2n}}, \qquad (7)$$

where the choice of neighborhoods is indexed $i = 1, 2, \ldots, C$ and dwellings $j = 1, 2, \ldots, N_i$. Equation (7) can be decomposed into a marginal and a joint probability statement, introducing nonlinear parameter σ. As a joint probability statement, this can be decomposed into:

$$\phi(j \mid i) = e^{\alpha_1 N_{1i}/(1-\sigma)} / e^{I_i} \qquad (8)$$

---

[14] See, for example, Anas [1982], McFadden [1978], and Maddala [1983].

[15] In the urban context Quigley [1982] proposes a more detailed hierarchy: choice of dwelling given neighborhood; then, choice of neighborhood given town; and finally, marginal choice of town.

and:

where:

$$\phi(i) = e^{\alpha_2 S_{2j} + (1-\sigma)I_i} \bigg/ \sum_j e^{\alpha_2 S_{2j} + (1-\sigma)I_j}, \tag{9}$$

$$I_i = \log \sum_{k=1}^{N_i} e^{\alpha_1 S_{1i}/(1-\sigma)}. \tag{10}$$

As with *MNL*, the *NMNL* parameters in α are derived through utility maximization principles, and are estimated with maximum likelihood methods. Parameter σ also provides an important generalization of the joint choice among structure and neighborhood. If $\sigma = 0$ then the choice model with *IIA* does indeed hold and neighborhood is irrelevant. If $\sigma = 1$, the choice of dwelling unit is dependent only on neighborhood attributes; all housing units within a neighborhood are viewed as identical.[16] Although the analysis above refers to a hierarchy in which neighborhood is chosen first, followed by dwelling unit within the neighborhood, the analysis is general and could be reversed and applied to test alternative hierarchies (e.g. structural attributes, then neighborhood) as well. Further work will be useful in evaluating the restrictions inherent in the more tractable *NMNL* analysis of structure and neighborhood, as opposed to the more general *MNL* model.

Ellickson [1981] provides an alternative formulation that is particularly useful in providing direct bids for local public goods. McFadden asks what type of dwelling and/or neighborhood m a consumer of type j is likely to occupy. Ellickson asks, instead, what type of consumer j is likely to occupy a dwelling of type m.[17] For any given dwelling, m, there will be a set of maximum bids from consumers of each type j. He uses a stochastic bid price function B_{mn} (for the nth consumer of type j) of the form;

$$B_{jn} = \xi_j(m) + \varepsilon_{jn}, \tag{11}$$

where $\xi_j(m)$ is the bid price function of the representative consumer

---

[16] Following Maddala [1983], as σ approaches 1, $\phi(j \mid i)$ approaches N_m/N, where N_m refers to the number of dwellings in the alternative neighborhoods, and N refers to the total number of dwellings in the market.

[17] This is perhaps the more "traditional" form of logit estimation, where the coefficients among choices vary, rather than the choices themselves. Maddala [1983] shows the algebraic equivalence of the two forms.

of type j, and ε_{jn} is a random disturbance term for type j consumers.
Ellickson seeks the largest bid from each consumer of type j such
that:

$$B_j^* = \xi_i(m) + \varepsilon_j^*, \tag{12}$$

where ε_j^* is the largest of all ε_{jn}. If the random variables ε_{jn} are
normally, lognormally, exponentially or logistically distributed, then
ε_j^* will have a Weibull distribution, the same distribution necessary
to estimate the McFadden model.

Whereas the McFadden model uses a set of alternative housing
choices among alternative locations to determine one set of
parameters, the Ellickson model uses the set of alternative buyers,
to estimate $(J - 1)$ sets of parameters among J types of buyers. The
Ellickson formulation does not solve the arbitrary nature of the
choice set (this time, the types of consumers, rather than the
alternative locations). Also, the necessary logit estimation may
involve an enormous number of parameters. For example, estimating the bid functions with 10 characteristics, over 12 classes of
consumers requires 110 parameters (10 characteristics multiplied by
11 classes—one class serves as the base). On the other hand, it is
intuitively pleasing, because the Weibull distribution, necessary for
estimating the equation, emerges endogenously from the
formulation.[18]

This section has discussed hedonic price and discrete choice
analysis, the two methods that are most often used for measuring
neighborhood effects. Hedonic price analysis became popular with
the availability of high speed multiple regression packages, and the
ability to handle large household-level data sets. Discrete choice
analysis required sophisticated computer algorithms that have only
recently become widely available and easy to use. With many of the
hardware and software problems solved, analysts should conduct
careful studies of the applicability and precision accorded by each
method in the measurement of neighborhood effects.

2.4. Demand for neighborhood attributes

The measurement of neighborhood effects on housing markets
suggests a market equilibrium involving both demand for and

---

[18] Zorn [1985] shows how this model can be used to relate population movement to
the capitalization of the local public sector into the price of housing.

supply of neighborhood components. With respect to demand, it is clear that neighborhood attributes enter household utility functions, as discussed in (6), similarly to other types of goods. The typical model of consumer choice appears to follow the Tiebout [1956] hypothesis in which households search among neighborhoods to find the one that meets their specifications. In these models, *voting with one's feet* replaces the market test (i.e. purchasing one good rather than another) that one usually associates with private goods. Property taxes usually function indirectly as user fees since the taxes are typically assumed to purchase larger amounts or different types of local public goods.

The Tiebout approach may apply to small suburbs, or to local neighborhood associations, with the binding covenants that are necessary to enforce certain regulations, or with organizational powers to provide local public goods, such as parks or swimming pools. It would seemingly omit neighborhoods, within larger jurisdictions, which are defined by race or ethnicity but which are not necessarily capable, either through increased taxes or through political power, to the manipulate public inputs to provide differential levels of public services.

Although early analysts were sanguine about identifying the underlying demand and supply parameters from hedonic price regression, recent analysis has shown the set of restrictions necessary for identifying either or both. As noted above, the hedonic price equation serves as the first stage of a two stage process in which the hedonic prices of individual attributes are determined. Figure 1 shows the set of equilibrium marginal bids and offers determined in the first stage hedonic price estimation. The second stage requires additional information to identify underlying bid (demand) and offer (supply) functions for any bundle component. Most of the exposition involves identification of structural components that are easily quantified, such as number of rooms, square feet or lot size.

Neighborhood components are not easily included in this characterization. Structural components such as lot size, number of rooms, living space are readily interpreted as scalar quantities within the housing bundle. One must ask, how attributes such as neighborhood safety, racial composition, or proximity to parks are to be interpreted. That is, should these neighborhood attributes be considered as *more* housing, or rather as externalities (similar to proximity to the central place u in the monocentric model) that enhance bids for land, or the structural components? The interpretation of neighborhood attributes yielding higher bids for structural components would seem to constitute a fundamental misspecification of the demand function, since the preference for neighborhood attributes (e.g. higher bid) is manifested here in an increased price for *non*-neighborhood attributes. It is shown below that such a misspecification biases price elasticities toward -1.0. Further, the interaction of the two types of components in a hedonic price model would suggest that the treatments of the two types of components should be symmetric.

2.5. Supply of neighborhood attributes

One of the earliest explicit economic analysis of neighborhood effects came in a supply context, through the examination of urban renewal by Davis and Whinston [1961], in which government intervention was justified through the externalities of the "Prisoner's Dilemma" model. The neighborhood effects, in this discussion, were external to the individual landlords; hence the landlords would not commit the optimal level of resources to renewal, without the others doing so. Since an urban renewal authority could internalize this neighborhood externality, the neighborhood effect would essentially be eliminated and optimal resource allocation would ensue.

Although the discussion is salient, it was never clear that the types of projects proposed for urban renewal really satisfied the Prisoner's Dilemma profitability criterion. That is, it was unclear that internalization of the externalities, through a governmental program (with the power of eminent domain), would make marginal activities profitable, and hence economically desirable. Moreover, unless eminent domain is both necessary (to neutralize strategic behavior by the last seller(s), who might hold their properties off the market) and available, it is not clear why private developers could not perform the same land acquisition and development functions as the government was expected to perform under urban renewal powers.

Also germane to the discussion of the supply of neighborhood attributes is a large literature on the costs of providing local public goods such as schools, parks, or hospitals.[19] This has customarily focused on the economies of scale, and by inference, on the optimal size for the public good production. Again, as discussed above, these are probably more applicable to small suburbs, where the decision process is more formally organized rather than a more amorphous neighborhood.

Still another interpretation of the supply of neighborhood attributes is discussed by Harrison and Rubinfeld [1978] and later by Freeman [1979]. In order to specify a second stage of the demand for neighborhood services in a hedonic price model (again, refer to Figure 1), it is necessary to make some assumption about the jointly estimated supply function. In a discussion of estimated impacts of air pollution regulations, Harrison and Rubinfeld suggest that the *supply of air pollution* at specific locations is not responsive to its impact on land or housing values (hedonic price). Freeman responds that in the longer term, quasi-rents attributable to clean air are related to the supply elasticity of housing construction in locations with clean air *rather* than the supply of elasticity of air pollution.

The literature on *quasi-public* goods, while most often employed in discussions of local public finance, provides useful insights into the supply of neighborhood attributes. Quasi-public goods, in this formulation, differ from traditional Samuelson-type public goods in two ways. First, the consumers do not demand the actual government-provided public good, but rather a localized version that is produced (with conventional production functions) using both governmental and private inputs. Second, different households (possibly in different locations) may have differing production functions for the quasi-public good. Neighborhood safety, for example, can be conceptualized as the output determined by a set of public inputs such as policemen, and a set of private inputs, such as locks on doors, burglar alarms and citizen patrols. Although the difference between public and private inputs may involve points on a continuum, consider, as before, all decisions internal to the household to be private, and the rest, including supply of public inputs, as well as neighbors' characteristics, to be public.

Following White [1979], characterize the dollar value of benefits

---

[19] Hirsch [1984, Ch. 9] provides a good conceptual discussion and review.

for the ith household from the kth quasi-public good as g_i^k, which is a function of public input x^k, private input a_i^k, and the vector of private inputs supplied by other households, $\bar{a}_j$, or:

$$g_i^k = g^{ik}(x^k, a_i^k, \bar{a}_j). \tag{13}$$

g^{ik} refers to the household's neighborhood production function. For the optimal allocation of resources to public (g_i^k) and private (c_i) goods, maximize the social welfare function, SWF:

$$SWF = W(U^i(g_i^k, c_i), \ldots) \tag{14}$$

over i individuals subject to resource constraint:

$$F(c_i, \ldots, a_i^k, \ldots, x^k, \ldots) = 0 \tag{15}$$

Maximizing (14) subject to (15) and (13) yields a generalized Samuelson condition for the optimal provision of a pure public good, requiring that the sum of the marginal benefits from the production of the quasi-public good using extra x^k equal the marginal resource cost of x^k, where the sum of the marginal benefits is derived from both the marginal utilities in the valuation of the quasi-public good, and from the varying efficiencies of households in producing it.

The public goods literature considers the substitution possibilities among the types of inputs into the quasi-public goods. White shows that the socially optimal levels of public and private inputs (and outputs) will be provided if there is non-strategic behavior on the part of the local government, if the government has no distributional objectives, and if the marginal utility of income equals unity for both the government and the consumers. If government officials act as monopolists in supplying some public inputs, using *Stackelberg manipulation*, the government will adjust these inputs according to private responsiveness. If private inputs are good substitutes in the production of g_i^k, or if demand for g_i^k is inelastic, production efficiency losses (in the former case) or consumer surplus losses (in the latter) are minimized.

The importance of this discussion for neighborhood is two-fold. Both market goods, and (neighboring) household producers *external* to the housing bundle, are important to the supply of neighborhood services that are received by the household. Moreover, the housing bundle (particularly the neighborhood services portion) can change over time, entirely due to external factors, such as the sociodemographic composition of the neighborhood, that are beyond the occupant's control. This type of analysis has had important policy implications over the recent past. In the late 1970s the United States Government moved from so-called *categorical* programs (funds tied to specific categories of aid) to *block grants,* which were geographically targeted, but subject to a much looser set of conditions. Among other objectives, the grants were designed explicitly to improve housing and neighborhood amenities *and* to promote neighborhood stability. It was quickly seen that any program that made neighborhoods more attractive, hence attracting inmovers, would both undermine neighborhood stability, *and* change the amount of quasi-public goods g_i^k received, through (13). Still further examples of neighborhood change are discussed below.

One final feature of the quasi-public good model is that it may support analysis of the premise (as is emphasized in the sociological and planning literature) that the neighborhood itself may provide a structure for the treatment of problems. If the residents recognize the externality, they may act in concert to alleviate it. This transforms the standard non-cooperative game (as noted by Davis and Whinston) into a cooperative game, where social pressure (e.g. neighborhood meetings or covenants) may be necessary for enforcement. The quasi-public good model would handle this nicely by allowing endogenous change in the production function for neighborhood.

2.6. Sociodemographic factors

Although the quasi-public good literature provides a helpful framework for relating neighborhood components to factors such as neighborhood safety or attractiveness, neighborhood character and stability are often defined (both by the public and by researchers) by race, class, income and ethnicity. With respect to the production technology, these represent *pure* public rather than *quasi-* public goods, since the possibilities of substitution in production are very limited. Although it could be argued that if the surrounding neighborhood were not to one's liking, one could put up high fences

or thick curtains so as to avoid it, these actions do not substitute for
a better neighborhood.

As noted in Section 2.2, there has been a substantial amount of
work on neighborhood effects in models of racial prejudice. The
model first proposed by Bailey [1957] provides a useful framework
for examining both the comparative statics and the dynamics of
neighborhood racial change. Bailey posits a border between black
and white neighborhoods, with housing identical among all neighborhoods. Three types (segregated black, segregated white, and
mixed) of neighborhoods emerge, with price patterns reflecting the
market preferences. If blacks prefer mixed neighborhoods and
whites prefer segregated neighborhoods, then housing prices will
be lowest in all—black neighborhoods, and highest in all—white
neighborhoods.

Kain and Quigley [1975] extend the model by considering supply
effects. Whereas Bailey's model is driven by consumer preferences,
Kain and Quigley propose that there may be sizable costs
(including subdivision of units, or construction of kitchens and
bathrooms) of converting housing units for new residents who may
have lower incomes, or tastes for different types of housing. These
conversion costs, which subsume various types of market frictions,
break the direct link between preferences and housing prices related
to neighborhood racial composition.

Kanemoto [1987] provides an excellent review of the literature
based on the monocentric model, and examines a model in which
whites receive externalities based both on size and proximity of the
black population, but blacks receive no racial externalities. In this
analysis, denoting the black-white border as u^* (with blacks living
between 0 and u^*, and whites living between u^* and city limit $\bar{u}$),
neighborhood racial stability requires that the boundary bid-rent
curve for blacks, $\partial R^b(u; u^*)/\partial u$, be at least as steep as that of
whites:

$$\partial R^b(u; u^*)/\partial u \leq \partial R^w(u; u^*)/\partial u. \qquad (16)$$

At the boundary, however, an increase in the black population
increases the externality faced by whites (i.e. the externality is both
closer and larger). If the external effect is very strong, the white
boundary bid-rent function may be steeper than the black function,
even though the underlying bid-rent functions may not be steeper.
This leads to neighborhood instability until the conditions above

(equation 16) are again met. If is apparent that this general set of sociodemographic neighborhood models, as noted by Kanemoto, awaits more detailed and rigorous analysis.

In the formulation above (which reflects the general literature), race (although class, ethnicity, or other demographic variables will do) is treated as an amenity, which is valued by whites, but not by blacks. Prejudices are treated solely in terms of tastes. In contrast, the *quasi-public* good format uses race as an input into *neighborhood*, which is valued within the utility function. In the quasi-public good model, whites and blacks may produce or value neighborhood differently. Moreover, the existence of a neighborhood production function suggests governmental policy instruments (i.e. inputs) directed toward the neighborhood *production function,* as substitutes.

The two approaches can be combined. Kanemoto implicitly uses the quasi-public good formulation, in an example of the impacts of upkeep externalities. Here, he considers the effect of [lack of] upkeep on the values of neighborhood buildings (among absentee landlords) to illustrate governmental policy inputs into the production of neighborhood services. Both Pigovian taxes and improved zoning and code enforcement influence the supply of private inputs into the neighborhood production function. More concentrated ownership allows a larger owner to internalize the externality, although Kanemoto recognizes the problem that renters lack the incentive to minimize maintenance costs.

In both the taste and the quasi-public good models (with the exception of the cooperative game), the individual's choice is based on parametric information; that is, he or she sees the neighborhood supply as defined by the sociodemographic factors discussed above, and expectations of change are typically not included. Neighborhood change (here, the change in the vector of sociodemographic variables), however, results from influx of new types of residents, and is determined by housing market conditions (excess demand and/or supply) in all neighborhoods. As a result, the demand for housing by some individuals in a specific area may lead to a decreased supply of neighborhood for others.[20]

---

[20] In this sense the externalities may imply nonconvexities in the modeling. These nonconvexities may lead either to the *nonexistence* of market equilibria, or to *multiple* equilibria.

The interaction of housing demand and neighborhood supply represents an extraordinarily difficult set of conditions to model analytically, and one of the only models with substantial experience in this format is the Urban Institute Simulation model (deLeeuw and Struyk, 1976). In a comparative statics framework, 90 households, with specified incomes and utility functions (which include race), relocate after a base line equilibrium has been disturbed. The solution algorithm requires that:

(a) each household maximize utility over available choices

(b) each dwelling either be occupied, or be vacant at a minimum (covering operating costs) price.

(c) total landlord profits be maximized subject to conditions (a) and (b).

(d) racial change from the initial set of proportions is minimized.

Condition (d) builds a history into the model. For model tractability, to avoid multiple solutions (brought on by similar housing and incomes, for example, in two areas), *ceteris paribus,* the solution that represents the smaller change from the previous pattern is preferred.

From the discussion above, it appears that the most fruitful avenue toward modelling this sociodemographic neighborhood behavior involves simulation models (see Anas, 1987, for a full treatment). Although such models became very popular for land use and transportation planning in the 1960s, with the collection of large data bases, and the availability of high-speed computers, they were almost devoid of behavioral specification, and their predictive power was weak. Further, even with large computers, they were almost prohibitively expensive to run.

Much of the fundamental analysis from monocentric models was developed to provide a strong theoretical base for analysis of urban land rents, transportation and housing patterns. The "real world," however, presents complications that are often analytically intractable. The analysis of racial prejudice in such an urban model is a prime example. Improved economic theory, and the plummeting costs of computing may help provide answers to the treatment of race and other sociodemographic neighborhood factors in urban housing markets.

2.7. Neighborhood comparative statics

The discussion thus far in this section has concentrated on the characterization of the equilibrium levels of neighborhood prices, and the demands for the supplies of neighborhood attributes. Within this discussion, I have alluded to the adjustments of prices and quantities, the comparative statics, to changes in the levels of neighborhood amenities. This section attempts a more systematic discussion of the comparative statics analysis.

At the household or dwelling unit level, attention has been focused on the measurement of neighborhood effects, and on the attempts to measure price impacts of external changes, such as transportation, environment, and land use. The presumption was that neighborhood effects "matter" if they are significantly linked to price changes. Yet, it is easy to provide a counter-example. Lind [1973] considers an area where half of the land parcels (*type* 1) are polluted and rent for R_1. The other half of the parcels (*type* 2) are not polluted and rent for price $R_2 = 2R_1$. If the polluted land is cleaned up, then the supply of unpolluted land has increased and a new price between R_1 and R_2 will be set. Suppose that the new price $R^* = (R_1 + R_2)/2$, so that aggregate land rents have stayed constant. Economic benefits have obviously occurred since the land is now more productive, but the aggregate value of the land rents is unchanged. Lind shows that the increased productivity is reflected both in changed market prices and in changed surpluses to the renters. Only if the surpluses are unchanged (and, most usefully, equal to 0 at both times) do the changed land rents reflect neighborhood effects.

Polinsky and Shavell [1976] provide a major interpretive clarification of the capitalization of amenities into land rents, in the urban context, by distinguishing between *small, open* cities (or parts of cities), and *closed* cities. Consider a project that enhances amenities at location k within a city. If that location is small relative to the rest of the city, then the utility level of the city can be taken as exogenous. Since residents at location k are temporarily better off than those elsewhere (with no locational price changes), migration into location k leads to increased land (housing) prices there.[21] Since the amount of land at the location is small compared

---

[21] Analogous to Lind's analysis, migration serves to eliminate surpluses.

to all of the land in the city, the increased amenity level does not change the overall city supply of land with the amenity, hence land values elsewhere stay the same. *Local* improvements, it would then follow, should increase *local* land and housing prices, and many empirical studies suggest that they do. There are numerous examples of transportation improvements, shoreline, commercial disamenities, or racial boundaries, all showing significant localized price effects.

In contrast, large scale improvements may lead to ambiguous results. Consider the construction of a subway system that halves travel time everywhere in the city. Suppose further that mobility is limited enough, that the level of residents' utility increases in this city, relative to other locations (the city is *closed*). The supply of accessible land has now increased such that the scarcity value (as in the example before) may fall. In the Lind context, surpluses have risen. Clearly there are economic benefits, yet attempts to measure them now require a general equilibrium model that accounts for the increased supply relative to the rest of the system (see, for example, Arnott, Pines and Sadka, 1986). As in the example above, the amenity improvement may not be reflected in land or housing values.

The general equilibrium requirement of the solution to the comparative statics problem has required analysts to characterize the processes of neighborhood change more carefully. One example is the longstanding wish to explain sudden shifts in neighborhood racial composition, often accompanied by changes in housing prices. This process is generally referred to as *neighborhood tipping,* and typically involves black succession into white neighborhoods. Anas [1980], while acknowledging that prejudicial factors may be present, uses a probabilistic framework to show how the inmigration of low income individuals can lead variously to rent increases or decreases, either smoothly, or with substantial discontinuities, depending on relative incomes, price elasticities, and sizes of the inmigration. The key to the analysis is the derivation of a possibly multi-peaked revenue function facing landlords, in a market with totally inelastic supply.

In this analysis, the landlord wish to maximize the profit function in neighborhood i:

$$\pi_i(\hat{R}_i) = \hat{R}_i \phi_{i1}(\hat{R}_i) + \hat{R}_i \phi_{i2}(\hat{R}_i), \tag{17a}$$

where π refers to profits, $\hat{R}_i$ refers to asking rent, and (ϕ_{i1}, ϕ_{i2}) are the probabilities (or by inference percentages) rented to class 1 or class 2 buyers (differentiated by income in this example). The probability functions (ϕ_{i1}, ϕ_{i2}) relate the demand from each group to total neighborhood supply. An additional constraint:

$$\phi_{i1} + \phi_{i2} \leq 1, \qquad (17b)$$

allows the possibility of positive (zero) expectations of vacancy (vacancy rate v) if $\phi_{i1} + \phi_{i2}$ is less than (equals) 1. If (17b) is binding, the actual revenue equals the asking rent with a probability of 1. If not, the actual revenue equals $\hat{R}_i$ with probability $(1 - v)$, and 0 with probability v. In this model, increased demand by individuals or increased numbers of the different types (here, races), lead to increased demand within the neighborhood. Anas is able to show how substantial discontinuities both in sociodemographic neighborhood structure and in the structure of rents can be generated, in a model that is driven by sociodemographic forces that are exogenous to the neighborhood.[22]

Strange [1987], in another promising recent development in general equilibrium neighborhood modeling, attempts to model explicitly the spatial interdependence of neighborhood activities. Reconsider the example in which there is an improvement in amenities at location k. In the traditional neighborhood model, all economic activities nearby react *independently* to that amenity improvement. Yet, it is also likely that these neighborhood economic activities would react to each other as well. Strange proposes a more general model with *overlapping neighborhoods,* and reaction functions for those who make economic decisions.

In this model, since neighborhoods overlap, the activities in one neighborhood will affect the opportunities and activities of someone else in the neighborhood. Using density as an example, an increase in an amenity at location k could have two possible effects on that area. It could lead to more dense development at location k, implying less dense development elsewhere. However, if wealthy

---

[22] Both Kanemoto [1987] and Miyao [1987] recognize the importance of racial prejudice, when analyzing the stability conditions of a model in which there are different household classes (most generally, black and white). Both find that equilibria become unstable the larger the reaction to the externality.

people react to the improvement with a demand for larger, *less* dense housing, the density could decrease, implying *more* dense development elsewhere. In either case, the precise impact at any distance from location k depends on the aggregate impacts through the reaction functions in all of the neighborhoods.

Ordering the reactions on either side of location k, one can characterize the set of reactions at distances $(k - n_k)$ through $(k + n_k)$ as Nash equilibrium solutions. Strange shows that the equilibrium is unique and globally stable (if the reactions to the amenity are small relative to the degree of neighborhood inter-dependence), but that estimating both the qualitative (direction) and the quantitative (size) effects is problematic. The only cases with unambiguous impacts require that the reaction functions be either all positive, negative or zero (the traditional case). This is clearly a promising line of inquiry, and the specification of different types and magnitudes of reaction functions should provide more guidance into the calculation of expected neighborhood effects.

The discussion above suggests a re-examination of the interpretation and measurement of neighborhood effects. Changes in amenities at location k trigger changes in activities, as well as changes in prices, elsewhere. It is clear that *zero* price effects might be observed, *not* because neighborhood effects are unimportant, but rather because the general equilibrium economic adjustments bring about offsetting supply and demand activity. Further, the existence and aggregation of reaction functions suggests a set of systematic impacts that can be modeled explicitly, rather than being treated, as in less sophisticated models, solely as random noise. Again, the characterization of such activity is a useful avenue for future research.

2.8. Discussion

This section has considered the measurement of neighborhood effects, and their characterization both through the individual and the market, and through the demand and the supply mechanisms. The theory and the measurement of neighborhood attributes are considered.

Both hedonic price and discrete choice analysis have been used to measure neighborhood effects and neighborhood preferences.

Although the research benefits from still another hedonic price, or discrete choice study are diminishing, rigorous comparisons between them are very desirable. The development of fast, inexpensive, and easy to use computational algorithms and statistical packages (for both mainframe and personal computers), will allow explicit testing of the two types of models against each other. These may still be hampered by data set inadequacies (discussed in Section 3), but the tools for the comparative analysis are available and the outcomes of such analyses will be helpful in model specification.

The most important theoretical work is the implementation of theoretical general equilibrium methods in ways that can be used for policy analysis. The overlapping neighborhoods model provides useful preliminary results, although the conditions for unambiguous impacts are very stringent. Further work on this problem, both theoretically, and with simulation models, where the solutions are either analytically intractable or ambiguous will be helpful.

The analysis in this section, with few exceptions, made little distinction between short term and long term individual, or market, behavior. It is clear, however, that the *transactions costs* of many activities can have important impacts on analytical results. Moving costs for consumers, or vacancy costs for landlords may have substantive effects on the modeling of the behavior of housing market participants. These concerns are addressed in Section 3.

3. SHORT RUN AND LONG RUN EQUILIBRIUM

The comparative statics analysis from the monocentric model generates a series of rents, housing prices, and residential locations that are stable in the long term, but not necessarily the short term. Dynamic analysis provides a steady state with constant rates of change. On the arguable, but useful, premise that there is some long term analytical regularity in land and housing markets, decisions that are viewed in the short term rather than in the long term provide analytical difficulties in empirical work.

Curiously, much of the literature on housing demand and supply implicitly regards consumer or producer decision in terms of single period efficiency conditions, even though the market frictions that face both demanders and suppliers are both well-known and hardly unexpected. Many articles on housing demand and on landlord behavior focus on recent (or *mover*) transactions which are presumed to be "closer to equilibrium" than are those which were consummated in the past. Recent movers are thought to be closer to their true demand curves than are those who have remained in the same residence for a long period of time. Similarly, on the landlord side, the charging of differential rents, and the acceptance of vacancies by the individual landlord who must presumably supply units inelastically in the short run, is at variance with simple myopic formulations, although consistent with longer term optimization.

Other monographs in this series address the issues of long run and short run equilibria and general urban structure in both comparative static and dynamic frameworks. This section addresses the distinction between the long run and the short run from the housing market perspective. The housing purchase itself may involve transactions and moving costs that can account for 10 percent or more of the house value, representing, either explicitly or implicitly, a year or more of housing expenses. No other household purchase suggests transactions costs of this level, and these estimates of transactions costs do *not* include time costs and out-of-pocket search costs. Similarly, from the supply perspective, a landlord has a constant, long term, relationship with the tenant (both in the renter and in the owner-occupant case) that is unusual in the study of the purchase of consumer goods (again the investment aspect of housing is ignored).[23]

In terms of the length and constancy of the relationship, the owner-occupant case is at once obvious and trivial, in that the landlord is renting to himself. Even here, however, the relationship is quite important for other analyses such as the user cost of housing, in which the untaxed implicit income represents a major owner subsidy. The renter case involves the tenant's decision whether to continue in the same location, and the landlord's gathering of information on tenant characteristics and costs pursuant to the decision as to whether to offer tenant specific discounts.

This section will examine supply and demand at the individual (rather than the *market*) level. It begins with a discussion of the

---

[23] Starr [1979] provides some useful discussion on this point.

measurement of housing prices in both the short term and the long term. It then considers both demand and supply behaviors, given transactions costs that may prevent easy adjustment to period-to-period economic changes.

Many of the problems related to the distinction between short term and long term behavior are manifested in econometric analysis. This will be treated within each section (price, demand and supply), as will some of the problems of empirical urban housing analysis related to issues of data availability. The final part of this section will consider the different implications of short term and long term analysis with regard to selected housing policies in the United States, Canada, and Western Europe.

3.1. Price measurement

The monocentric model discussed in Section 2 generates a unit price for housing services that is fundamentally related to land rents, yet the empirical application of this theory can be difficult. In the monocentric model, since land rents decrease with distance from the downtown, so, too, must housing prices, which are a function of the share of land in the production of housing. If land, for example, constitutes 20 percent of the value of a housing parcel, then a 30 percent fall in land price (due to decreased accessibility) leads to a 6 percent (30 percent of 20 percent) fall in housing price.[24]

Theoretically, this monocentric formulation is elegant and useful, since the rent function, typically obtained by solving a first order differential equation, readily generates a housing price function. The measurement of housing prices in this manner, however, presents profound problems. It is very difficult to find urban land parcels without major encumbrances, neighborhood effects, or differential tax treatments so that "pure" land values may be measured. In addition, land's share in the housing bundle is often arbitrarily determined as 5, 10 or 20 percent, depending on the author and the context of the analysis.

---

[24] This example assumes unitary elasticity of substitution in production, typically a Cobb-Douglas production function. Alternative functions weaken the maintained assumptions of constant budget shares but do not affect the conclusion that housing prices must fall with land prices.

Most economists have come to measure housing prices with the hedonic price analysis of housing bundles, as noted in Section 2. For j different submarkets at time t, the hedonic function (1) can be rewritten as:

$$R = R_{jt}(S, N, u), \tag{18}$$

where, as above, S and N refer to structural and neighborhood characteristics, and u refers to a set of location-determined parameters including distance and/or commuting time to employment (usually downtown) centers, and differential tax burden. Defining an index bundle (S^*, N^*), one then evaluates its price according to the different functions R_{jt}, and at various levels of u. R_{jt}^*, then, is the price of a unit of housing at u within submarket j, at time t.

The hedonic price model generates a short run equilibrium, which implies that there are *no* zero-profit constraints on the suppliers of housing services. In other words, long run equilibrium is *not* necessary for a solution to occur, and the resulting indices represent short run equilibrium values which will differ, in theory, and in measurement, from those generated by long run equilibrium models. Further, large positive or negative quasi-rents (e.g., for attributes that are no longer being built, but are found on existing stock) can exist in a housing market, and may persist until the market adjustments that would (in the long run) drive them to zero overcome the transactions costs of performing them. (See, for example, Kain and Quigley, 1975).

The index defined in (18) is consistent with the monocentric model, in defining housing in terms of quantity and location (indirectly through its price). A logical and important alternative to the use of such a one-dimensional characterization of housing quantity, would involve specification of supply and demand for each component n_i or s_i within the bundle. Since the hedonic prices are jointly determined by supply and demand, it would be necessary to estimate and to identify $2(k_s + k_n)$ underlying supply and demand equations (for k_s structural components and k_n neighborhood components), subject to adding-up conditions, and requiring nonlinear or separate (among markets) hedonic price equations. The econometric difficulties posed here (Epple, 1987) have proven to be extraordinarily difficult.

Analysts have chosen to reduce the scope of the problem in two ways. For example, those looking at environmental amenities, such as pollution, choose a small subset of the vector N and hold all else equal (Freeman, 1979). Alternatively, they arbitrarily group components (either heuristically, or with data reduction methods) weighted by their hedonic prices into *characteristics*, often termed, *quality, quantity, neighborhood,* or *services* (see, for example, King, 1973). These have proven to be more tractable, but the results are often quite sensitive to the specific formulation used.[25]

Finally, the price indices represent *estimates* rather than parameters, as they are are derived from *imputed,* rather than explicit prices. Even the best hedonic estimates explain no more than 80 percent of the variance in observed bundle prices (which is an excellent result in cross-section econometrics), and the hedonic prices of individual components have generally been less stable than desired (Goodman, 1978). This instability, as noted in Section 2, is largely due to component multicollinearity and is particularly troublesome in attempting to estimate demand functions for the components themselves. Although overall fits remain good over time and space, the variations in implicit prices seem far larger than would normally be expected from the theoretical hedonic housing price model.

The unexplained variation indicates divergence in the price upon settlement between the buyer and the seller, from the "true" market price. If the true market price is P^*, then, for the ith transaction in submarket j at time t, observed price $\hat{P}_{ijt} = P^*_{ijt} + (e_i^T + e_{ijt})$, where e_i^T refers to a transaction-specific error, and e_{ijt} to measurement error in the estimating equation. Since the price levels for individual units are not known with certainty, some transactions may be consummated at prices that represent good or bad buys for the buyers or sellers, yielding error component e_i^T. Irrespective of e_{ijt}, a positive (negative) value of e_i^T implies lower (higher) quantity of housing than was actually purchased, when the total expenditures are known exactly. There are also some interest-

---

[25] Consider the distinction between housing quantity and quality. The first bathroom may be considered quantity, but the second and subsequent bathrooms might be treated as quality, as might be features such as fireplaces and hardwood floors. The arbitrary nature of the classification provides problems in interpreting results.

ing econometric problems from the measurement of long term price with error. These are considered in more detail in Section 3.2.3.a.

3.2. Demand analysis

3.2.1. Importance of transactions costs

As noted above, the change in housing quantity purchased requires transactions costs that are much larger, in both absolute and percentage terms than other goods. Search and moving costs, for both owners and renters, and substantial closing costs (for owners) suggest that the quantity decision requires intertemporal optimization to amortize the costs over a longer period. This is important in the interpretation of the theory of housing demand, the modeling of tenure choice, and the econometric measurement of demand elasticities. It also suggests that limiting samples to movers, on the premise that they are closest to equilibrium, is generally an inappropriate procedure in demand estimation.

This section considers a simple intertemporal utility maximization model with special attention to housing demand, and it emphasizes the transactions costs of moving. In this model, the consumer has perfect foresight with respect to income, and to the prices of housing and all other goods. Due to liquidity constraints, she is unable to borrow perfectly against expected future income (modeled here as total inability to borrow), and she starts in renter (smaller) housing. She must decide *at time* 0 when, or whether, to move, from renter (typically smaller) housing to owner (typically larger) housing.

Many of the key analytical points with reference to the moving transactions costs can be made with a two (rather than necessarily a multi-) period model. Let long term utility U, a function of housing, $h = (h_1, h_2)$, and everything else, $c = (c_1, c_2)$, be the sum of current period (U^1) and discounted future (U^2) utility:

$$U = U^1(h_1, c_1) + \rho U^2(h_2, c_2) \qquad (19)$$

Incomes y_1 and y_2 are known, as are the set of housing prices (p_1, p_2), the price of everything else (normalized as 1), discount factor ρ, and transactions cost t_r.

Transactions costs (see Hirshleifer, 1976) limit household flexibility. The decision to increase housing consumption in period 2 is accompanied by transactions costs which may involve both *lump sum* (search and moving) and *proportional* (closing costs are usually related to the total housing expenditure $p_i h_i$) components. For ease of exposition, I consider only the lump sum component. At time 0, the consumer is faced with two streams of disposable income, depending on her decision whether to move, between periods 1 and 2. Regime *I* (moving) provides:

$$y_1 = p_1 h_1 + c_1, \quad \text{in period 1, and} \quad y_2 - t_r = p_2 h_2 + c_2, \quad \text{in period 2.}$$
$$\text{(20a)}$$

Regime *II* (*not* moving) provides:

$$y_1 = p_1 \bar{h} + c_1, \quad \text{in period 1, and} \quad y_2 = p_2 \bar{h} + c_2, \quad \text{in period 2,}$$
$$\text{(20b)}$$

where $\bar{h}$ refers to the constrained $(h_1 = h_2 = \bar{h})$ housing purchase in each period.

To solve the problem it is necessary to maximise (19) separately with respect to (20a) and to (20b), and to compare the resulting utilities U_I^* and U_{II}^{**} (where single (*) and double (**) *asterisks* refer to the optima under Regimes *I* and *II*). The consumer moves (stays) if U_I^* is greater (less) than U_{II}^{**}, or:

$$U^1(h_1^*, c_1^*) + \rho U^2(h_2^*, c_2^*) \gtreqless U^1(\bar{h}^{**}, c_1^{**}) + \rho U^2(\bar{h}^{**}, c_2^{**}) \quad \text{(20c)}$$

Because of the non-local nature of the problem, a geometric treatment is useful. Consider the set of choices described in Figure 2, representing both increasing income $(y_1 < y_2)$ and decreasing housing price $(p_1 > p_2)$ from period 1 to period 2. If transactions cost t_r equals 0, the consumer plans to purchase more of both h and c in period 2 (than in period 1), moving from A to B. With positive t_r, the opportunity set (the second period budget constraint in 20a) shifts inward, as noted by the dashed line.

If t_r is large enough (as is shown in Figure 2), the consumer chooses Regime *II* instead of Regime *I*. A large enough value of t_r, in Regime *I*, cuts disposable income such that the consumer can not even reach indifference curve U^1 (where she would be if she did not move and did not change her purchases of h or c) in period 2. As such, she is better off under Regime *II* (not moving) than under

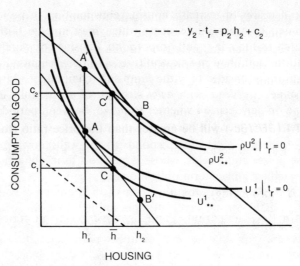

FIGURE 2   Two-period optimization with transaction.

Regime *I* (moving), since under *II* she could purchase more c_2 than is provided at A, the optimum reached according to y_1, p_1, and U^1 (the period 1 conditions). By staying in the original location, she can achieve points A and A'.[26]

By optimizing *over* the *two periods*, she can do even better than that. Although (19) can be maximized (see Goodman and Kawai, 1985) with respect to the income constraints (equation 20b) from Regime *II* ($h_1 = h_2 = \bar{h}$), it is instructive to make the immobility constraint more explicit, as:

$$\mathcal{L} = U^1(h_1, c_1) + \rho U^2(h_2, c_2)$$
$$+ \lambda_1(y_1 - p_1 h_1 - c_1) + \lambda_2(y_2 - p_2 h_2 - c_2) + \lambda_3(h_1 - h_2), \quad (21)$$

with the LaGrange multipliers referring to the two income constraints (λ_1 and λ_2) and the immobility constraint (λ_3).

Optimizing with respect to h_1, h_2, c_1 and c_2, given the decision not to move, yields:

$$(\partial U^1/\partial c_1)[((\partial U^1/\partial h_1)/(\partial U^1/\partial c_1)) - p_1] = \lambda_3$$
$$= -\rho(\partial U^2/\partial c_2)[((\partial U^2/\partial h_2)/(\partial U^2/\partial c_2)) - p_2], \quad (22)$$

---

[26] Similarly, by optimizing according to second period income and price conditions, she could achieve B and B'.

where λ_3 measures the foregone utility from the requirement that h_2 equal h_1. Since $-\rho \partial U^2/\partial c_2 < 0$, the marginal rate of substitution must be greater than the price ratio in one period, and less than the price ratio in the other (ignoring the possibility that the immobility constraint is not binding, i.e. $\lambda_3 = 0$). If $y_1 = y_2$, $p_2 < p_1$, and housing is a normal good, then $(\partial U^1/\partial h_1)/(\partial U^1/\partial c_1)$ will be less than the price ratio (too much housing) in period 1 and $(\partial U^2/\partial h_2)/(\partial U^2/\partial c_2)$ will be greater than the price ratio (too little housing) in period 2. This corresponds to the well-known example of "house-poor" households, whose large short term obligations are offset by smaller longer term obligations.

From Figure 2 (noting the lower set of indifference curves, U^1_{**} and ρU^2_{**}, and housing level $\bar{h}$), this implies that the consumer must adjust to the *second best* conditions (caused by the moving costs) by accepting a lower level of utility than dictated by *current* economic conditions in period 1, in return for a higher level in period 2. Hence, points C and C' are chosen (with respect to $\bar{h}$, c_1, and c_2), rather than A and A', or B and B'. By inference, this suggests that evaluating (20c), the utilities under alternative regimes, is equivalent to comparing the sizes of transactions cost t_r, and the marginal cost (in terms of the forgone utility from being constrained to the same quantity of h in both periods) λ_3. That is, $U^*_I \gtrless U^{**}_{II}$, as $\lambda_3 \gtrless t_r$.

Although a two period model imposes restrictions (e.g. the transactions costs must be amortized in one period), it emphasizes several features that are important for empirical work. First, the equating of current price ratios, to ratios of marginal utilities (i.e., single period efficient conditions), an assumption that is crucial to the assertion that movers alone are in (or closest to) equilibrium, is highly restrictive. This condition is highly unlikely to be met in a multi-period optimization. As a result, the assertion that movers are closer to equilibrium can not be justified. This is entirely separate from perceived *censored sample* econometric problems of simultaneity between moving (and/or tenure choice) and housing demand (suggesting two stage procedures, such as those proposed by Heckman, 1979), but is related instead to the underlying theory of consumer optimization itself. Rather than limiting the estimation to recent movers, one would sooner argue that as a first approximation, there should be a healthy distribution to households over many different lengths of residency.

Second, conventional cross-section methods, looking at *present* prices, and *present* incomes (as opposed to representations of the longer term vectors of incomes and prices) will almost certainly underestimate long term income and price elasticities. The permanent income hypothesis, proposed first by Friedman [1957], decomposes current income into permanent (long term) and transitory components. Since housing consumption should respond to variations in permanent income, and since the variance of current income is decomposed into the variance of both the permanent and the transitory components, it is easy to show (Goodman and Kawai, 1982) that without the proper instruments (which essentially impose intertemporal conditions), estimated permanent income elasticity will be biased toward zero.

Third, one can also reinterpret the discussion of equations (19)–(22) to look at tenure-specific estimates of housing demand. Let Period 1 refer to the time *before* a given move (typically renting), and Period 2 refer to the time *after* the move (typically owning). In this situation, the high transactions costs hinder marginal changes in consumption. As a result, *given* tenure (here 1 refers to renting, 2 to owning), measured changes are biased toward zero. This suggests (again, apart from econometric problems) that tenure-specific estimates are also likely to bias the measured price and income elasticities downward.

Even using panel data, similar econometric problems may obtain since analysts are unable to measure the consumers' full horizons.[27] If it were possible to discern the horizons, one could "average out" the adjustments from one location to the next, and compare them to similarly treated changes in income. However, data limitations typically require the measurement of adjustments over shorter periods (e.g. one year). These adjustments show most households being *totally unresponsive* to income changes, with a few being *very* responsive since it is their year to adjust, according to long term parameters. Although, in the aggregate, expenditures may change predictably, without improved modeling and information, individual

---

[27] These problems require two-stage modeling of the (discrete choice) mobility decision, and the housing demand, conditional on the mobility decision. Analysts have recognized this, but the modeling, variable specification, and estimation are all still rudimentary.

responses, especially among owner-occupants (who move at very
low rates), may appear almost random.
  Consider a household with 3 members (e.g. a couple and a child).
They live in a 2 bedroom apartment. Incomes go up by small real
percentages for a year or two, but the household does not increase
housing consumption (i.e. does not move). The mistaken inference
is a very low income elasticity; the more appropriate inference
involves the saving for a larger unit, and the friction of the
transactions cost, again compared to the disutility that comes from
the constraint that housing be consumed in the same location. The
theory, as described here and elsewhere,[28] is well developed, and
provides important analytical insights. The important research to be
performed involves the improved availability of panel data, and
econometric techniques to perform the necessary long term
analysis.

3.2.2. Renting and owning

With the possible exception of automobiles, housing is the only
market that maintains large (in both size and market share) owner
and renter components. Unlike automobile users, most households
rent *and* own at various times in their lives, and the ownership
decision involves not only consumption of services, but ownership
of a large asset. This section looks at the recent changes that have
occurred among the rental and the owner housing stock. It then
looks in more detail at the tenure choice decision, with special
attention to the role played in the short and in the long term by
expectations of housing price inflation.

a. Owner and renter markets.   Housing services are among the few
goods that support both substantial owner and renter markets. As
mentioned above, the move between residences often involves a
tenure choice as well. This involves a decision not only to purchase
services but also to own an asset which may account for a
substantial proportion of the household's wealth.
  The tenure choice decision has several distinguishing aspects.

---

[28] One of the first explicit microeconomic treatments of this topic was Muth [1974].
For other discussions, see Friedman and Weinberg [1982], Hanushek and Quigley
[1979], Goodman and Kawai [1985], and Olsen [1987].

1) Out-of-pocket costs for owners (particularly with level payment mortgages) are more certain.

2) In North America and Western Europe owner housing is usually larger (providing more space), and often higher quality housing.

3) The imputed rental income is generally untaxed.

4) Nominal interest payments and real estate taxes (in the United States) are deductible from taxable income.

5) The asset is subject to substantial capital gains, that are explicitly (Canada) or essentially (due to tax deferral policies in the United States) untaxed.

Although the tax considerations are certainly important, they are not crucial to the tenure choice discussion. Canada, for example, has had a much less favorable tax treatment for housing (vis. deductibility of mortgage interest payments), yet Canadian determinants of tenure choice and housing price patterns have been very similar to the United States.

Traditionally (at least in North America) there has been a sharp distinction between the characteristics of the owner and renter housing stocks. Renter housing has generally been multi-unit housing; owner-occupied housing has generally been single-family housing. Ownership has been decentralized, and Sternlieb [1966] and others have found no better than normal landlord profits in most cases into the 1970s. The 1970s saw a deterioration in the rental housing market. Despite some striking exceptions (high quality rental housing in locations such as New York, Washington or San Francisco), rental price indices fell precipitously, relative to all other prices, from 1970 to 1980.

This is evident in comparing gross rents, which increased by 89.8 percent, to the entire Consumer Price Index which increased by 112.9 percent, over the ten year period. Since rental housing is also included in the CPI, the true difference (between rental housing and all other goods) must be substantially larger.[29] Lowry [1981] contends that the fall in real rents may be overstated in that it did

---

[29] The treatment of housing (inclusion of owner-occupied prices and nominal interest payments) in the CPI tended to overstate both the increases in the CPI and the cost of housing. Nonetheless, most estimates of rent indices relative to the overall change in consumer prices, support the conclusions stated here.

not account for depreciation of the dwelling units, yet even his adjustment increases the rental price increase to 102.7 percent. Under these cricumstances, and given other institutional problems such as the actual or threatened rent control in many locations (which would dampen investment), it is hard to argue that rental housing capital represented a competitive investment.

Although ownership of capital is more properly discussed in a thorough treatment of wealth distribution, which is far beyond the scope of this monograph, conversion of residential capital from renter to owner status is important in an urban context. While the return to unsubsidized rental housing was falling in the early the 1970s, owner-occupied housing was rising in price. The result was the conversion of renter units (particularly small units) from renter to owner units. The 1980 Housing Census estimates 2.13 million condominium-coop units (they did not merit a separate category in 1970). This was followed in the early 1980s by an unprecedented conversion of owner units (particularly single family units) to renter units. Many owner-occupiers who wished to move elsewhere were unwilling to take unexpected capital losses when interest rates of 14 to 16 percent (or more) were capitalized into house prices.

b. User costs.   This unwillingness to take capital losses should be interpreted in the context of *housing user cost,* which treats expected appreciation, property taxes, income taxes, and depreciation of the asset as factors that influence the cost of using housing capital. User cost was derived to reconcile the strong housing demand of the mid-1970s with the unprecedented high nominal interest rates of that period. During this period, these interest rates were offset with growing marginal income tax rates and expected asset appreciation; user costs, as a result, stayed low, and in some years were even negative (see, for example, Dougherty and Van Order, 1982).[30]

User cost can be formulated to address both the consumption and the investment aspects of the housing decision. The standard formulation implies consumption only. Expected capital gains on housing are a major determinant in the derivation of user cost.

---

[30] Rosen [1979] presents an excellent study of the impacts of federal income tax rates for the United States.

Consider the relationship between the rental rate on a housing asset
R, and its asset value V. (The notation follows Mills and Hamilton,
1984.) Ignoring property taxes and depreciation, the cost of housing
capital, R can be written as:

$$R = [(r + p^e)(1 - t_i) - (g^r + p^e)]V \qquad (23a)$$

where r is the real rate of interest, p^e is the expected inflation rate,
t_i is the marginal income tax rate, and g^r is the expected real rate of
capital gains. The model reflects the fact that in the United States,
capital gains from the sale of owner-occupied housing are essentially
untaxed.

Equation (23a) can be rearranged to discuss the movement
between owner and renter statuses.

$$V = R/[(r + p^e)(1 - t_i) - (g^r + p^e)] \qquad (23b)$$

Clearly, expectations of capital gains change the denominator. If
these expectations are optimistic (high g^r) and if the costs of
converting renter to owner housing are small, this would suggest the
capitalization of these gains in selling the house. It also explains
some of the movement by consumers from renter to condominium
or to cooperative housing. Conversely, a small or negative value of
g^r explains both the reluctance of movers from 1981 to 1983 to sell
their homes, and their decsion to become landlords, at least in the
short term.

An early examination of user costs actually treated the tenure
choice as a function of expected mobility, rather than expected
mobility as a function of tenure choice. Shelton [1968] calculated
break-even lengths of stay with respect to transactions and closing
costs, for owning and renting. Using conditions germane to the
mid-1960s, he found that if one were planning to live in the same
dwelling for more (less) than 3.5 years, it would be preferable to
own (rent), since the longer expected stay would amortize the high
transactions costs of moving. Updates of these calculations for the
late 1970s (with large expected appreciation in the owner-occupied
market) lowered these break-even numbers considerably.

Most studies have examined tenure choice in consumption terms.
In other words, if a consumer wishes to purchase h units of
housing, which tenure is cheaper? The fact that the dwelling unit is

a viable investment (and for some, the only investment) is generally not considered. User cost is used in this analysis as well.

Plaut [1987] integrates portfolio aspects of the housing purchase with housing consumption in a model similar to (23a) that makes the timing of the tenure change endogenous. The household rents (and accumulates savings) from birth to time t^*, which is determined endogenously. At t^* it purchases housing stock H, which provides $h(H)$ services until death. No moves are permitted, once the house is purchased. The household optimizes over a fixed horizon, with assets either in housing or in an alternative financial asset. (Borrowing or short positions are not allowed).

For a risk averse household, volatility in housing prices has both a *wealth effect* and a *price effect*. Increased housing price volatility, relative to the financial asset, leads to later purchase of housing (to shorten the period with exposure to the more volatile asset), as well as to less housing both for investment *and* consumption (i.e. lower demand). Corner solutions to the problem (i.e., either buying immediately, or not at all) are also permitted, and have natural interpretations.

Since rental moves are not prohibited by this model, moving costs are implicitly zero among rental housing units, and infinite for owner housing. Alternative formulations might be appropriate. It would also be desirable to make the number and the timing of moves endogenous within the model; some of the literature on the formation and lengths of contracts might prove useful. In cases of this type, the model also serves as a portfolio allocation model for the supply of housing capital, comparing housing capital to the alternative assets, and giving a useful descrption of the move between the allocations of housing and other capital.

For empirical work, as with the simple microeconomic model above, modeling of expectations is both very important, and at this time, very unsophisticated. The formation of housing price expectations in this circumstance is largely unstudied. Housing price expectations are typically treated as recent averages of local or regional housing price increases. Examination of rational expectations assumptions for the empirical work would be useful. Whereas much of the theory assumes perfect (or at least pretty good) foresight as to market conditions, it is apparent from the experience of savings and loan organizations (who should have had the most experience) that foresight over at least the past twenty-five years has been far from perfect.[31]

3.2.3. Empirical findings

a. Econometrics. One of the fundamental problems in measuring individual housing market behavior, is the difficulty (particularly with cross-section data) in interpreting currently observed prices or incomes in a long term context. The more recent availability of panel data (following individual households over time) alleviates this problem to some extent, but the long lengths of residence at given locations, and the substantial transactions costs in moving, lead to uncertainty as to whether or how the currently observed parameters should be treated. Much of the econometric work has involved examining the problems of estimation when variables are short term in nature, and constructing instruments to represent the appropriate long term variables.

Empirical work on the difference between long term and short term housing demand behavior has proceeded along two related paths. The first has involved academic research into the determinants of housing demand, focusing on the measurement of price, income, and interest rates. The second has involved a sympathetic federal government response (since the 1970s) to the arguments of economists that income subsidies were not only more efficient than prices subsidies, but would actually lead to substantial increases in housing demand. The Experimental Housing Allowance Program (EHAP) was developed to test the various impacts of proposed changes in public program changes with respect to housing. It is discussed in detail in Section 3.4.[32]

Both of these research paths built on the strong aggregate analyses of Muth, Reid and others, who found demand price elasticities of approximately −1.0 and income elasticities greater

---

[31] At this time, winter 1988, many lenders still have mortgages of 5 and 6 percent on their books. For this reason (as well as many others) many savings and loan organizations became technically bankrupt during the early 1980s, with liabilities far outstripping assets.

[32] Hundreds of working papers, reports and evaluations of the EHAP research have been written. The discussion here, and later in the text will, of necessity, be cursory. Two very good summary volumes are Bradbury and Downs [1982] and Friedman and Weinberg [1982].

than $+1.0$, and as high as $+2.0$. Repeated analyses using individual data (Mayo, 1981, provides a good summary) found absolute values for both elasticities to be less than $+1.0$ and most of the analyses from EHAP project found them to be closer to 0.0 than to 1.0. Much of the analysis of econometric bias in housing demand analysis results from application of standard *errors-in-variables* methods. Polinsky (1977) addresses these concerns in a spatial context by examining both aggregation biases, and estimation problems in a spatial setting. Many of the early housing demand studies used aggregate data at the census tract or block group level. Polinsky shows how such aggregation tends to internalize the variance among individuals. If this internalized variance is interpreted as transitory income, the resulting mean incomes might yield results that approximate those that would be obtained using permanent income.

He also explains the estimation problems due to the correlation of price and income (price (income) falling (rising) with distance to the downtown, consistent with equation 3). Increased income leads to increased housing purchases, but the outward move implies lower housing prices. If the housing price elasticity is between 0 and -1.0 the lower prices imply lower expenditures and income elasticities (measured by expenditures). Remedying this problem requires explicit spatial variation in the measured price (early analyses omitted this variable, or asserted that it did not vary). Many researchers (e.g. Polinsky and Ellwood, 1979) have addressed this problem, and verified Polinsky's conjecture.

I address, in this section, the problems linked to the distinction between short term and long term optimization. Consider again the analysis implied by (19)–(22), involving intertemporal optimization. It is evident that measures of long term income and long term price are necessary in this context, to estimate price and income elasticities consistently. Due to the transactions and search costs of moving, random shocks in income streams or in relative prices will have negligible effects on demand. Empirical analyses have focused on the formulation of statistical instruments for these price and income terms.

The econometric treatment of income is a straightforward adaptation of the *errors-in-variables* problem where current income, Y, is used as a proxy for the appropriate variable, permanent income,

Y^P.[33] If $Y = Y^P + Y^T$, (Y^T is transitory income, uncorrelated with permanent income) then the appropriate regression is:

$$H = \alpha_P Y^P + \alpha_T Y^T + \beta P + \varepsilon_0. \tag{24a}$$

Consider the misspecified regression:

$$H = \alpha Y + \beta P + \varepsilon_1, \tag{24b}$$

where $\varepsilon_1 = (\alpha_P - \alpha)Y^P + (\alpha_T - \alpha)Y^T + \varepsilon_0$. If all of the standard least squares properties hold, then $\hat{\alpha}$ is a weighted average (Goodman and Kawai, 1982) of the true coefficients α_P and α_T, with the weights corresponding to the relative shares of the variance of Y contributed by each of its two components. Since α_P is likely to be larger than α_T (which is often restricted to 0), misinterpretation of the short term Y as the long term Y^P will lead to a downward bias in estimates of permanent income elasticity.[34] Other income measurement problems occur in the specification of permanent income through the use of sociodemographic variables. This problem is addressed in Section 4.4.3.

The econometrics of price must be treated in two parts. The first involves estimation errors in the derived price variable. In an econometric sense, this departs from the usual problem of errors-in-variables. Whereas errors-in-variables, as noted above, typically leads to estimation biases toward 0 (since part of the variance in the explanatory variable is error rather than true variance), in housing demand models, the price elasticities here are biased toward -1.0. This stems intuitively from the fact that since total expenditures are exact, errors in estimation of the price term are inversely related to errors in the quantity term.

This is most easily seen in the demand equation in which

$$\log H = \beta \log P + \varepsilon, \tag{25a}$$

(with all other variables and all subscripts suppressed). Adding

---

[33] Here, and in all subsequent discussion of econometric specification problems, regression variables will be noted with capital letters.

[34] Goodman and Kawai [1982] also address the correlation of income and price in this context. They find price and *transitory* income, rather than *permanent* income, to be correlated. Hence Polinsky's omitted variable problem may lead to inconsistent estimates of the impacts of both price and transitory income.

$\log P$ to both sides yields logarithm of total expenditures E_x:

$$\log E_x \equiv \log P + \log H, \quad \text{or} \quad \log E_x = (1 + \beta) \log P + \varepsilon. \quad (25b)$$

When estimating:

$$\log E_x = b \log P^* + \varepsilon', \quad (26)$$

the fitted value $\log P^*$ from a hedonic regression may measure $\log P$ with error, i.e. $\log P^* = \log P + w$. Denoting the respective variances of P and w as σ_P^2 and σ_w^2, respectively, *errors-in-variables* analysis shows that $\hat{b} = b/[1 + (\sigma_P^2/\sigma_w^2)]$, implying that the coefficient of P^*, is biased toward 0. It follows then that β is biased toward -1.0.

A *different* bias is seen with misspecification of the long run price term, particularly if samples are restricted to movers. Rather than the random variation, which would bias elasticities toward -1.0, there has been considerable evidence (e.g. Follain and Malpezzi, 1979, Marshall and Guasch, 1983, Goodman and Kawai, 1985) that prices decline *systematically* with length of residence, either because of level payment mortgages (which decline in an inflationary economy) or due to renter discounts. The length of residency discount can be modeled as $l_r = \delta_0 + \delta_1 t_m$, where t_m refers to length of residence.[35]

If rational movers anticipate the discount, then the true regression equation for recent movers is:

$$H_i = \beta \log(P_i - l_r) + \varepsilon_i. \quad (27a)$$

If the sample is restricted to movers, (especially in cross-section data) one observes P_i rather than the appropriate long term price $(P_i - l_r)$, and the resulting regression will be misspecified as:

$$H_i = \beta \log(P_i) + \varepsilon_i', \quad (27b)$$

where:

$$\varepsilon_i' = \varepsilon_i + [\log(P_i - l_r) - \log P_i]. \quad (27c)$$

It is easily shown that $\hat{\beta} < \beta$, since the covariance of $[\log P_i - l_r) - \log P_i]$ and $\log P_i$ is positive, and:

$$p\lim \hat{\beta} = \beta\{1 + [\text{Cov}(\log(P - l_r) - \log P), \log P]/\text{Var}(\log P)\} \quad (28)$$

---

[35] δ_0 is sometimes referred to as a "sitting discount," unrelated to length of residence. The analysis holds if $l_r > 0$.

In this case, then, (i.e. mover families only) estimated price elasticities will be biased away from zero.[36]

The empirical implications for demand estimation involve several aspects. First, there must be more sophisticated modeling of the mobility decision, because this is largely where housing quantity adjustments take place. Quigley and Weinberg [1977] derive a simple model that suggests the comparative statics conditions necessary for individuals to move, but it is necessary to put this model in a framework that asks when, within the life-cycle, the family chooses to do so. Henderson and Ioannides [1984] develop a model to estimate *spells* or residency, in a treatment that is similar to the analysis of unemployment spells in the labor economics literature. Housing adjustment occurs (generally) when moving from one spell to the next. Even with panel data, however, it is difficult to see more than one spell at a time. Conceptually, at the very least, *two* spells would be necessary, with the appropriate permanent income and price terms linking the *mid-points* of the two spells.

The mobility decision must have a significant effect on the proper measurement of income and price. If a household plans on moving within a year, then expected price changes for their current unit are irrelevant. If the household plans to remain in the unit for some time, then the price and income effects assume more importance in the household's mobility calculation. Similar arguments obtain with permanent income or wealth. Both of these interact significantly with the income and property tax effects (see Olsen, 1987).

Finally, the problems of mobility and transactions costs may provide a bridge between the traditionally high income and price elasticities of the aggregate data estimates, and the lower elasticities of the estimates using individual observations. In the aggregate, one sees the changes in demand (omitting depreciation and renovation) of the 20 percent of the population that moves each year (a figure that, for the United States, has been remarkably constant; see Rossi and Shlay, 1982). Those that make big changes (after overcoming the transactions costs) are combined with the larger group that makes no changes. If the underlying mobility deter-

---

[36] Even using a linear form, which yields covariance of 0, the intercept, and hence the elasticity, is biased away from 0.

minants do not change, these aggregate elasticities may be appropriate for several purposes. Microeconomic analysts who interpret the monocentric model as a *long run equilibrium model,* may argue that the aggregate elasticities are useful since "everyone" moves in the long run. Macroeconomic analysts wishing to predict the impacts of macroeconomic and tax policies on housing aggregates may also find the aggregate elasticities useful.

They are *not,* however, useful for examining, either theoretically or empirically, localized (within an urban area) short term adjustments to changed incomes and/or transportation costs. Utilization in this way for analysis and/or prediction would be appropriate only if the long term adjustment could be decomposed into a set of short term adjustments; transactions costs make this unrealistic. Nor are the aggregate elasticities appropriate for predicting individual household responses to housing assistance programs. Such programs, no matter how permanent or expected, can not offset the discreteness in the process of the housing adjustment, brought about by transactions costs and mobility constraints.

b. Data bases. A final concern in this section involves the microeconomic data necessary to estimate the demand functions, with special reference to the difference between the long and the short term. The ideal data set should be (1) panel data for both owners and renters over a substantial time period (10 years or more), with (2) good urban geographic detail, (3) neighborhood specification, and (4) income, wealth and tax information. From this perspective, the optimal data set would be a suitably chosen sample of Federal Income Tax returns, with appropriate geographic identifiers. This would avoid the practice of imputing marginal tax rates by assumption, and would indicate individuals' long term tax and investment planning decisions. Attempts to formulate such data sets have been (and are likely to remain) unsuccessful.

The requirements (particularly those of a spatial nature, which could make respondent identification easier) lead to severe problems with respondent confidentiality constraints. The American (formerly Annual) Housing Survey (AHS) contains panel data which follows the *house* rather than the consumer. It also provides very limited geographic detail and poor neighborhood specification. The Panel Study on Income Dynamics fulfills requirement (1) better, but its coverage of (2) and (3) is also weak. Numerous researchers have collected cross-sectional data sets of house sales for many metropolitan areas, which are typically self-selecting (owner-occupied housing, which is sold through realtors' Multiple Listings Services, is usually of better quality than the average housing), and which, unlike the American Housing Survey, preclude replication across metropolitan areas. The ideal household data collection project would be neither cheap nor easy to collect, maintain, and manipulate, but it would be necessary to examine many of the long term housing demand questions that are limited by current data availability.

3.3. Housing suppliers

The housing supply decision is very much affected by the unmalleable nature (houses can last hundreds of years) of the capital good, leading to significant transactions costs in either converting it (to provide more or fewer services) or demolishing it to produce a new unit. Moreover, symmetric with the demanders, landlords also face search costs with respect to new tenants, and opportunity costs with respect to possible vacancies. This section begins with the role of housing supply in the monocentric model and then distinguishes between short and long term supply elasticities. Models of landlord optimization are then followed by a discussion of the vacancies and abandonment that may result.

3.3.1. Monocentric model

The monocentric model, as discussed above, provides a rather passive role for housing suppliers. Given the downward sloping land-rent gradient, with constant cost of capital, suppliers substitute land for capital as distance from the downtown increases. Land is developed outward, with downward sloping rent and housing price functions and without vacancies (which presumably, in long run equilibrium, would not exist if the markets were clearing properly, since any landlord would prefer to rent for any positive return, rather than zero earned for the vacancy). There is no explicit difference between owning and renting; indeed all of the analyses in the monocentric model assume renter housing.

As with housing demand, transactions costs drive an important wedge into the model for housing suppliers. Demand-related transactions costs involve the costs facing consumers in adjusting to desired demand. Supply-related transactions, on the other hand, involve the suppliers' adjustment costs in adjusting to factor and product prices. The simplest example might involve the subdivision of housing. Consider a dwelling unit with eight rooms, including six *generic* (i.e. providing living space only) rooms, one kitchen and one bathroom. If the landlord wishes to divide the unit into two units, he must provide an additional bathroom and kitchen. The additional plumbing, wiring and appliances constitute adjustment costs to changed product and factor prices. Other examples include demolition and clearing costs, both of which hamper landlord adjustments to changes in the economic environment.

Following McDonald [1979], consider the capital structure of urban housing. His substantive analysis follows a first period land rent gradient, which is developed according to the monocentric model (equation 2). Suppose then, for example, that the population increases, thus increasing demand. This changes rents everywhere, and the city expands into previously unused agricultural land at the border. Consider units at the border (i.e. those just *inside,* which were developed at time $t = 0$, and those just *outside,* to be developed at time $t = 1$). Those units that are just outside the original border (determined by the urban land rents and the exogenously determined agricultural land rents) would be built according to the usual marginal productivity conditions with respect to land, that is:

$$p_{h1}(\partial H/\partial L_{11}) = R_1, \qquad (29)$$

where H is output, L_{11} is land first developed at time 1, p_{h1} is the price or housing built at time 1, and R_1 is land rent at time 1. In contrast, the land that is only marginally closer to the downtown, with the same rent R_1 is redeveloped only if:

$$p_{h1}(\partial H/\partial L_{11}) - \Delta_{10} > p_{h0}(\partial H/\partial L_{10}). \qquad (30)$$

L_{10} refers to the land at time 1 that was first developed at time 0, and Δ_{10} refers to the *demolition cost* at time 1 of land developed at time 0. The new rent gradient R_1 is presumably higher than R_0, and equation (30) would be equivalent to (29) *if* adjustment were costless (i.e. $\Delta = 0$). Since it is not, the link between land rent, and housing capital-land ratios (hence, housing supply) is broken. With this set of costly adjustment processes, it is easy to show how units can be left vacant or be abandoned since the costs of converting them to other use may be greater than the gains from doing so.

This section will examine housing supply in the short run (in contrast to the longer run decisions) in general terms, and will then examine specific supplier and landlord behavior. I will consider decision rules and pricing policies that have become apparent among landlords. Many of them are predicated on the fact that the landlord/tenant relationship is long lived and (often) personal, and that there are major transactions costs that may forestall the discrete changes that must occur when either wants to adjust.

3.3.2. Long term and short run supply elasticities

In contrast to the plethora of research on housing demand, there is much less work on housing supply, particularly in the short run.[37] This section outlines briefly the discussion of both long and short run elasticities, and reiterates an observation made by Olsen [1987] that the marginal gains to research in housing supply are substantial indeed.

There is a rather general consensus among housing analysts that in the long run (all factor prices variable), the supply elasticity for housing services is very large, if not infinite. The earliest systematic analysis (Muth, 1968) observed that neither building material prices nor construction wage rates seemed to vary with the rate of new residential construction. Moreover, there seemed to be a high level of both entry and exit within the home-building industry. Both of these are consistent with constant non-land (largely capital) costs (along with falling land costs, which, as noted in Section 2.1 comprise but a small share of the factor costs) in the production of housing stock, and by implication, housing services. Estimating the elasticity of substitution between land and captial to be 0.75, and land's share relative to nonland factors to be 0.05, Muth infers a housing supply elasticity of +14.0. Follain [1979] verifies this in time-series aggregate data. Stover [1986] estimates cost functions,

---

[37] McDonald [1979, Ch. 4] provides a detailed review of urban housing supply models. Olsen [1987] also surveys housing supply.

using disaggregated data (at the metropolitan level) to estimate a cost function. He, too, is unable to reject the null hypothesis that the price elasticity of supply is infinite. This analysis is equivalent to the discussion in (29) and (30), with Δ (in the long run) equal to 0. It has become clear, however, that since shorter term values of Δ are positive, short run elasticities may be considerably smaller. For example, landlords can not immediately withdraw capital stock from an area in which rent control has been imposed. Programs to provide income subsidies for the purchase of housing may become transfers to landlords, if local housing supply is inelastic. I return to this point below.

Ozanne and Struyk [1978], in several pieces pursuant to the development of the Urban Institute model, attempted to measure supply elasticities by following units over a 10 year period. Their resulting elasticities are thus short run in nature, since it is difficult to interpret data that is arbitrarily collected every ten years as representing long run equilibrium. Using a constant elasticity of substitution production function, with initial stock, labor, and capital as inputs, and a profit function considering both current and future (discounted) returns, they derive the supply function:

$$h = \alpha h_0 + \theta [p_s(n)/\mu(w)]^\gamma, \qquad (31)$$

where h_0 (h) is the initial (end of period) level of services, α is the fraction of initial housing services remaining at the end of the period, $p_s(n)$ is the price per unit of housing services in neighborhood n, $\mu(w)$ is the weighted average of factor prices, θ is a parameter incorporating effects of expectations and returns to scale, and γ involves substitution elasticities and returns to scale.

They estimate the model with survey data from the Components of Inventory Change (CINCH) survey, which follows individual dwelling units. Several data deficiencies are acknowledged, which reflect general problems with data sets of these types. Bundle specifications omit several important structure and neighborhood characteristics. Second, *stock,* rather than *services* is used in the estimation. Nonetheless, they delineate lower and upper bounds of supply elasticity for housing services (owner and renter elasticities are about the same) of 0.3 and 1.5, respectively. Replication of these estimates with more recent data (most particularly, taking advantage of the underused AHS) is an important item on the agenda for housing researchers.

3.3.3. Landlord optimization

The general discussions of supply decisions, to this point, have abstracted from the microeconomic decisions made by the suppliers of housing services, both owner-occupiers and landlords. Both the availability of improved data in the AHS, and increased interest in renter analysis (particularly through recent governmental attempts to cut costs in housing subsidies with increased reliance on cash subsidies for the rental housing market) have led to improved analysis of the renter housing market. The textbook treatment of the housing market would show each landlord as a price taker who adjusts rents with the market each period (typically a year). Yet, repeated hedonic price analysis has shown length of residence discounts of between 0.5 and 2.0 (and as much as 2.5) percent per year of residence. Goodman and Kawai [1985] find mean discounts for sitting renters (those staying in the same unit) in several metropolitan areas of 5.0 percent or more. In some places (New York, Boston, Los Angeles) through the late 1970s, these may have reflected rent control legislation, but the pattern is too pervasive (Follain and Malpezzi, 1979, Marshall and Guasch, 1983) to be explained solely by rent control.[38]

Consider a simple intertemporal model of landlord behavior. Assume that the landlord is able to plan future maintenance and management expenses, based on expectations of tenant "wear and tear" of the unit. However, the landlord does not know, when taking on a new tenant, what types of expenses the tenant will generate. Since the maintenance and management expenses are fixed, the landlord can maximize his return by maximizing net revenue, i.e. total revenues less tenant-specific costs, net of the fixed costs.

In this model, the landlord deals with both new and old tenants. "Good" tenants imply operating costs Z_1; "bad" tenants imply operating costs Z_2, with $Z_2 > Z_1$. Changing tenants is costly, with

---

[38] Both Follain and Malpezzi (40 cities), and Goodman and Kawai (19 cities) find rent discounts to be significant in analyses where separate regressions are estimated for each housing market.

cost E, which could include both search costs and/or the opportunity costs of a vacancy, if a new tenant can not be found. By the end of the first lease (for convenience, one year), the landlord has gained enough information on tenant characteristics to know whether the tenant is good or bad. For a variety of reasons (changes in job, family size, or incomes, for example), tenants may move from period to period, staying at the previous location with probability ϕ, which is a function of the bundle price but is unknown to the landlord. Given the search costs that may be necessary to attract new tenants (who may be either good *or* bad), the landlord may benefit by providing a small incentive (thus increasing ϕ) to keep the good tenants in the unit, and by charging a premium to drive out the bad ones.

Letting, ϕ_i equal the probability (under regime i) that the tenant will accept the discount l_r (as discussed above, with respect to specification of housing demand), expected profits are π_1 if length of residence discounts are offered, and π_2 otherwise. Variable p is the market price of housing to new buyers, h is the quantity of housing services, and l_r is the discount offered:[39]

$$\pi_1 = [\phi_1(p - l_r)h - \phi_1 Z_1] + (1 - \phi_1)ph - (1 - \phi_1)(E + Z_2) \quad (32a)$$

$$\pi_2 = ph - \phi_2 Z_1 - (1 - \phi_2)(E + Z_2). \quad (32b)$$

Given the fixed costs, the landlord chooses the price setting behavior so as to maximize π_i. Regime π_1 is preferable to π_2 ($\pi_1 > \pi_2$) if:

$$l_r h < [1 - (\phi_2/\phi_1)][E + (Z_2 - Z_1)]. \quad (33)$$

Since $\phi_1 > \phi_2$, and $Z_2 > Z_1$, the right hand side is positive. The landlord then offers the discount if the discount is less than the expected increase in tenant costs, i.e. search costs for a new tenant plus the differential costs between old tenants and new tenants ($Z_2 - Z_1$). The new tenant may not necessarily be bad, although monitoring costs (even for a good tenant) for the first year would account for costs Z_2 rather than Z_1.[40]

---

[39] As noted in the text, if the tenant is truly bad, the landlord might wish to raise asking price well above p.

[40] A negative value for l_r would indicate a model for "rent gouging," where in the face of search and moving costs for the consumer, a landlord tries to appropriate some of the occupant's consumer surplus.

Equations (32a) and (32b) are also consistent with a model in which the landlord picks prices from a random draw, but tenants buy only if the price landlord's offer is less than or equal to the true price. In such a model, no tenant will pay more than the market price (assuming zero moving costs), and discounts will be correlated with length of residency. This model is discussed further in Section 3.4, in a policy context.

Although the discussion above considers equilibrium for an individual landlord, market equilibrium is less apparent since units are renting for different prices. Börsch-Supan [1986] examines equilibrium in a market where there is search by both buyers (for units) and sellers (for tenants). He formulates a two period model in which landlords and tenants must have heterogeneous characteristics, and then demonstrates the necessary conditions for equilibrium. For equilibrium to exist, at least one of the two groups (landlord or tenants) must be uncertain of the characteristics of the other at the beginning of the first period. Second, there must be free migration of tenants among housing markets to guarantee steady state heterogeneous distributions of tenants among landlords.

3.3.4. Vacancies and abandonment

The monocentric model has little to say about unused housing units, since in the long run prices should adjust to clear the market for all unused units. Unused housing within urban areas involves either vacant or abandoned units. One could argue that due to search and transactions costs, a smoothly-functioning housing market requires some positive vacancy level, so that occupants and residences can be matched in some optimal way. One can draw a useful analogy with the labor market analysis of the optimal rate of unemployment, given the search costs involved in matching workers with jobs.

The model of landlord behavior sketched above (equations 32–33) shows how landlords can accept vacancies as a result of optimizing behavior. Landlords may incur vacancies, since E can be interpreted both as search costs for new tenants, and/or the opportunity cost of a vacancy. Anas [1980], in the model of neighborhood tipping discussed in Section 2.7, also shows how landlords may maximize revenues by setting rents above market clearing prices, again resulting in vacancies. Since the vacancies reflect disparities between the offers of sellers and the bids of buyers one would expect them to be short term and (in the absence of alternative motives such as speculation) random in nature. *Abandoned* (hence vacant) dwellings follow as the end results of the transactions (demolition) costs in the adjustment of housing capital to changed factor costs and demand conditions (equation 30). In a sense, long term vacancy evolves into abandonment, if the bids necessary to operate the unit profitably are not forthcoming, and the costs are too high to convert the unit to an alternative use.

There has been little analysis, however, of an *optimal vacancy rate,* in terms of the percentage of units left vacant as the result of short run failure to rent individual units. Policy analysts often state than vacancy rates of less than 5 percent indicate housing market tightness (irrespective of trends in housing prices), and government housing assistance programs also measure tightness (and compare it across metropolitan areas) in terms of vacancy rates. Yet, the statistics such as those collected in the decennial Census are often unable to distinguish between vacant units and abandoned units. Consequently urban programs targeted to remove abandoned housing (which may have no economic value), may be interpreted as lowering the vacancy rates to unacceptable levels.

3.3.5. Empirical work

Literature on landlord behavior has been brief and incomplete. For owner-occupiers, it is difficult to separate the consumption of housing from the self-supply of housing services. Landlord data, on an individual level, have been difficult to obtain, due either to the segmented nature of the sector (hundreds of thousands of entrepreneurs) for small entrepreneurs, or to confidentiality (disclosure) problems for big ones.

Porell [1985] uses the AHS to address the impact of owner- or manager-occupancy on the quality of housing services in rental dwelling units. The common supposition is that the *pride of home ownership* leads the resident landlords to provide better services either through increased inputs due to the low evaluation of one's own time, or through the more careful screening of tenants. Porell's empirical results are mixed; small structures (four or fewer units) seem to benefit from owner or residency management (with 30 percent fewer deficiencies). For large structures, it is impossible to distinguish between landlord/manager residency, and other explanatory factors such as consumer, neighborhood, or building characteristics.

Mayer [1985] addresses landlord's rehabilitation investment decisions, with particular attention to loan availability and the resident-nonresident status of the landlord. He measures neighborhood loan availability as the *percentage share* of all sales of residential properties financed from commercial banks and savings and loans (measured at the census tract level). An increase from 1 standard deviation below, to one standard deviation above the mean for loan availability, increases the likelihood of rehabilitation by about 50 percent. Mayer is more sanguine than is Porell about the salutary effects of landlord residency; occupant landlords appear to make more repairs; and to invest with less regard for the composition of the neighborhood.

Engle and Marshall [1982] perform one of the few microeconometric studies of vacancies. They argue that since a vacancy results from a bid price that falls short of the offer price, one can examine the determinants of vacancies in terms of this probability. The probability that a unit will be vacant equals the probability that the landlord's rent offer, R^o is greater than the bid R^b. If the R^o and R^b for unit i composed of components X_i are characterized as:

$$\log R_i^o = X_i \beta^o + u_i^o, \tag{34a}$$

and:

$$\log R_i^b = X_i \beta^b + u_i^b. \tag{34b}$$

The vacancy probability is then calculated as:

$$P(R_i^o > R_i^b) = \Phi X_i (\beta^o - \beta^b)/\sigma_e, \tag{35}$$

where σ_e is the standard error of the difference of the error terms u_i^o and u_i^b, and Φ is the cumulative normal distribution function. The resulting probit regression (whose coefficients are related to the differences between the bids and the offers), finds no systematic relationship of unit vacancy to observable characteristics.

As noted above, further theoretical and empirical work is necessary on landlord behavior, and on vacancy and abandonment.

Much of the discussion of landlord behavior is either highly theoretical, or (as noted by Mayer and Porell, for example) rather impressionistic. The theory should acknowledge that many landlords are small scale capitalists, with limited access to outside funds, who may have only a few units (hence fearing vacancy) and who may place small valuations on their own time. Theoretical work is also necessary in distinguishing between vacancies as random events, or as systematic occurrences, implying later abandonment. Longer term vacancies suggest that asking prices (with the given market conditions) are too high to match the unit to a renter.[41] Abandonment suggests that the market prices are too low to earn a positive return in the current use, and that alternative uses do not provide sufficient profits to make acquisition and demolition attractive.

The analysis of empirical data on landlord behavior is in its infancy. Data sources such as the American Housing Survey allow researchers to follow dwelling units over time. The public data files available from the EHAP Supply Experiment contain an enormous amount of data on landlord maintenance activities, and should also support substantive research.

3.4. Implications for policy analysis

The distinction between long and short term behaviors has critical importance in the evaluation of governmental programs to provide housing assistance. There are both economic and political considerations in any analysis and evaluation. The prediction of economic phenomena, as noted thus far in this section, often depends on the adjustment period posited, since it is important to measure both short and long term impacts properly.

There is also a political concern if short term impacts are considerably smaller than are long terms ones. Housing programs may be judged as unsuccessful, either according to speed of impact (i.e. the improvements do not occur quickly enough) or magnitude of impact (i.e. the perceived improvements are not large enough).

The focus of governmental housing programs (in the United

---

[41] As argued earlier, shorter term vacancies may result from positive search costs on the parts of both landlords and tenants.

States) over the past 50 years has evolved from the building and operating of public housing, to the consideration of cash equivalent income transfers (Olsen, 1982, provides a good summary and discussion). In housing programs, as with food stamps, political considerations prohibit actual cash payments for housing.[42] Economists have supported the proposal that housing programs should resemble income transfers, with the conventional microeconomic analysis showing unrestricted cash payments to be superior to payments in kind.

The theory was buttressed, in the 1960s, with studies that found income elasticities to be between +1.0 and +2.0 (deLeeuw, 1972). Not only, then, were income transfers superior on theoretical grounds, but they would lead to large increases in housing consumption as well. The counterargument was that such programs at local levels would lead to rent inflation. Landlords would raise rents to appropriate the transfers for themselves. The transfer payments would, due to inelastically-supplied inner city housing, go to inner city landlords, through the hands of inner city tenants. Proponents implicitly expected the high long run demand and supply elasticities discussed above. Opponents implicitly expected lower short term supply elasticities that would lead to increased prices. Little discussion was directed to distinctions between long and short term behaviors.

The major test of these supply and demand effects was the Experimental Housing Allowance Plan (EHAP) of the 1970s which had a demand component, a supply component and an administrative activity component (not discussed here). The demand component involved a sophisticated menu of subsidies, including percent of income and percent of rent subsidies, provided to selected households over six cities for a three year period. The supply component involved *saturation* (providing money to all who qualified) of two housing markets over a ten year period, to determine both aggregate demand responses, and supply responses to the program regulations and to the increased market prices.

Two points relate directly to the discussion in this section. First,

---

[42] Economists might argue that cash payments would increase well-being, even if the aid served as a substitute for other resources, and hence did not materially increase consumption of food or housing; their argument would probably not be politically persuasive.

estimated demand elasticities (both price and income) in the EHAP were much lower than expected (significantly less than 1, under all circumstances, and often less than 0.5, in absolute value). Many analysts have argued that either adjustment periods were not long enough, or that the changes were not viewed as permanent. Second, supply elasticities, as inferred from the price increases in the two areas served by the supply experiment, appear to be high enough to absorb the increased demand with little price inflation. It has been variously suggested that this result was due either to slow adjustment in demand, to unexpectedly low participation rates or to peculiarities of the two study sites (Green Bay, Wisconsin and South Bend, Indiana) themselves.

It is apparent that the moving and transactions costs of the supplier and demander decisions will serve to confound evaluation of such programs. Returning to the analysis summarized in Figure 2, if the transactions costs of moving are large, then increased incomes will lead households to buy more c_1 and c_2 (the alternative goods) rather than more housing, *not* because their long term housing demand is necessarily inelastic, but rather because they are optimizing in the long term and have already acted according to a prior set of expectations. Landlords and developers most likely also optimize according to long term (rather than short term) constraints with respect to rent increases, vacancies and maintenance.

Evaluation of housing programs of other types, and in other places, also benefits from the distinction between the short run and the long run. Börsch-Supan considers West German tenant rent- and eviction-control legislation, in an analysis that recognizes the need for *second best* criteria, when both moving costs (for tenants) and differential operating costs by tenant type (for landlords) are present.[43] He finds that the restrictions lead to rents that are higher than without the restrictions, but that neither tenants' well-being (utility) nor landlord's profits need be lower than in the unrestricted case (given the second best circumstances). The higher rents offset higher moving costs for the tenant; the landlord can appropriate some of the tenant's higher utility in the form of the increased rents.

---

[43] The West German *Law for the Protection of Tenants from Arbitrary Eviction* basically prohibits tenant eviction, and indexes the rent once the tenant has moved in. When a tenant moves, the rent can be freely set.

In summary, responses to changed prices and/or incomes are less elastic in the short term than in the long term, although most analysts have come to feel that the high demand elasticity estimates of the 1960s can not be matched using household data. Arguments that long term adjustment has not taken place at the time of measurement are usually irrefutable, and perhaps irrelevant, since one can argue in response that long term programs are not always long term.

The major research dictated by the differentiation between the short and the long run is related largely to econometric considerations. Multi-period optimization on the parts of either buyers or sellers is understood theoretically, but it is very difficult to achieve econometrically. Problems of censored samples, among suppliers and demanders, require improved econometric techniques. Empirical modeling of household expectations is rudimentary at this point and will also require more sophisticated modeling. Finally, it is crucial to collect and to maintain long term panels of data, with good urban geographic detail, for tracing both household and landlord behaviors.

4. DEMOGRAPHIC VARIABLES

Like many other subfields of microeconomics, urban housing analysis has presented little explicit treatment of demographic variables. Few would disagree that large families may consume more, or that blacks may consume less, at least in part because of discrimination. Nonetheless, much of the discussion and modeling have been rather *ad hoc* in their treatment of demographic indicators. As before, I emphasize the microeconomic aspects of demographic variables, as opposed to time series treatment of aggregates.

This section will address the implications of demographic variables in both the larger market context, and in the context of individual choice. Demographic variables (that is, household size, marital status and other long-term decisions), except where explicitly noted, will be treated as exogenous to the model. Along the same lines, the term *demographic* will essentially refer to all non-price and non-income terms in the analysis.[44] The section is divided into portions looking at the *market effects* of demographic variables, followed by the treatment of *household-level* demographics. The *market* section first looks at the treatment of demographics in the monocentric model, then in terms of households and *headship,* and lastly, in terms of neighborhood effects such as *gentrification.*

The *household* section examines the inclusion of demographics in the journey-to-work literature, and also in the tenure choice decision. It then considers the more general formulation of demographic effects in the estimation of individual demand equations. The section ends with special reference to racial effects, and a discussion of the difficulty in distinguishing between racial discrimination and tastes.

4.1. The monocentric model

The determination of locational equilibrium was discussed in the context of monocentric model in Section 2. Recall the derivation of a rent gradient from locational equilibrium condition (2) in which the marginal cost of commuting is traded against the savings in the cost of land or housing. The positive transportation costs make it more expensive to live away from the downtown, which is where all households (each one having 1 worker/member) are assumed to work. When the model is closed, it derives individual housing supply and housing demand at each distance u, out to the edge of the city, $\bar{u}$.

The only explicit treatment of demographic variables in this model comes through the formulation of the individual housing demand equation, and its impact on city size. Market demand S_D at each location u is written as:

$$S_D(u) = n_p(u)s_D(u), \qquad (36)$$

---

[44] The term *demographic* has also been used by scholars studying determinants of population size, including fertility or mortality. While one can argue (as is done in Section 4.4.2) that over the long term, *all* of these factors are endogenous to the model, this exposition will use *demographic* to refer to the non-price, non-income terms.

where s_D refers to demand per household and $n_p(u)$ is the number of households. The market demand is equated to market supply to determine jointly $p(u)$ and $S_D(u)$. Supply may be characterized either as malleable capital (i.e. zero transformation [conversion and/or demolition costs] costs) or as vintage capital (positive transformation costs) following McDonald [1979].

Individual demand is formulated with a constant elasticity demand function:

$$s_D(u) = Ap(u)^{\eta_p} y^{\eta_y}, \qquad (37)$$

where $p(u)$ refers to housing price at distance u, y to income, and η_p and η_y to the relevant elasticities. Closing the model requires that:

$$\int_0^{\bar{u}} n_p(u) \, du = N_p. \qquad (38)$$

Equation (38) is an "adding up" condition that the sum of individuals residing from the central business district ($u = 0$) out to distance $\bar{u}$ add up to total population N_p.

Thus, increases in N_p, determine exogenously (although they may be endogenous within systems of cities), increase housing demand, and hence city size. Mills [1972] performs extensive analysis of the malleable capital model by varying the coefficients. Demographic characteristics can influence the model through the constant term A of the individual demand curve (which is subsumed in the formulation of the equilibrium rent gradient) and the results are straightforward. That is, with malleable capital, any non-price factor that increases (decreases) housing demand leads to the geographic expansion (contraction) of the city through equation (38). Similar analyses occur with vintage capital (McDonald, 1979), although the degrees of expansion and contraction depend on the sizes of the transformation costs.

A more important role for demographic variables emerges through the discussion of leisure (more broadly, the intrafamily allocation of time to *non-market*) activities, as first proposed by Becker [1965], and elaborated by Muth [1969]. In equations (1)–(3) above, valuation of leisure time is crucial in the determination of locational equilibrium in the monocentric model. Increased wages lead to both higher demand for housing *and* higher valuation of leisure time. If the income elasticity of housing demand is greater (less) than the income elasticity of leisure time valuation, the household will move further (closer) to the central workplace. By comparing the valuations of leisure time between family members (White, 1977), or by interpreting leisure activities more broadly as *non-market activities,* aspects of the intra-family allocation of time are readily included. Hochman and Ofek [1977] following Gronau [1974, 1976], show how family size (i.e. number of children) and number of market workers can influence the household location in extensions of the monocentric model. Differing rent gradients and locations, by family type, are derived.

A third treatment of demographic variables in monocentric models involves racial discrimination. Two types of discussions refer to urban settings. The first refers to a set of border models, following Bailey, which were the first to treat discrimination in an explicitly spatial setting. This type of model were then grafted onto the monocentric model with explicit reference to rent gradients and spatial equilibrium.

The standard treatment (for example, Courant and Yinger, 1977, Kanemoto, 1987) was discussed in Section 2. In these models, racial discrimination (a function of increased percent white) typically reduces the amounts of housing received by whites, and increases the amounts received by blacks. Differing bid-rent functions are then derived for both groups and market equilibrium conditions are characterized. Most of the tractable solutions to the models lead either to complete integration or to complete segregation by race. Other attempts to explain social issues in urban spatial structure with respect to race have been less successful. Yinger [1976], for example, tries to explain the locations and shapes of ghettos using the "minimum border" hypothesis (i.e., ghettos form so as to minimize the border between whites and blacks). His argument is disproved by Loury [1977], who shows that the ghettos that would form according to the "minimum border" hypothesis would be located on the outskirts, rather than in the centers of the cities.

4.2. Families and headship

It should be abundantly clear that family formation and growth have substantive impacts on urban housing markets. The most salient example seems to occur and recur with the cyclic impacts of the generation of post-World War II "baby boom" children. Clearly, housing demand, and the demand for other family-related items jumped after World War II, with the return of servicemen, the rise in income compared to the Depression of the 1930s, and the formation and growth of new households. The adulthood of the "baby boomers" influenced the housing market again in the 1970s and early 1980s, as they formed their own households, leading both to large numbers of new households, and decreased sizes of existing ones.

Although most consumer models assume household size to be exogenous, economists have recently become more interested in the factors influencing *headship,* the formation of households. Headship influences the housing market through the demand for separate units. It may also have spatial consequences (migration to the surburbs, for example) if new dwelling units must be built to accommodate the increase in numbers of households.

The standard housing demand model treats the household size as given, yet the 1970s (in the United States and Canada) saw the number of new households increase by 16.94 million in the United States (1.69 million in Canada), or 26.7 (28.0 in Canada) percent. Household size in the United States fell by more than 10 percent (on average) from approximately 3.20 to 2.82, and in many urban neighborhoods (where there had been big families with many children) household size fell by more than 0.5 persons per family.

Goodman and Taylor [1983] document this in detail for a specific urban area. Not only household size, but household *composition,* as well, had impacts on housing and on community services. In many neighborhoods in Baltimore, numbers of school-aged children fell by more than 1 child per household. One well-publicized result has been the closing of many elementary schools due to lack of students.

Although standard housing market analysis treats household size as exogenous, studies of "headship" treat household size and household formation as endogenous. Smith [1984], for example, uses time-series analysis to estimate Canadian headship rates as functions of disposable income, user cost of housing, availability of public housing and socioeconomic variables. The dependent variable is number of households per 100 members of the population.

Higher housing user cost relative to income is negatively related to the rate of headship, especially among younger nonfamily (single-person households and households of unrelated persons) households. Börsch-Supan [1988] attempts a cross-sectional treatment of headship. He first splits conventional families into *nuclei,* defined as married couples or single individuals, together with all of the children below age 18. Children older than 18 are considered as grown-up, and form new nuclei even if they (still) live in their parents' homes. Older adults, living with their children, are also considered to be separate nuclei. The analysis uses the nuclei as units of observation, and then allows each nucleus to decide among all possible alternatives *including* living arrangements in another existing household, or living as an independent household. Concentrating on young and elderly singles, he finds (using the AHS) headship rates to be negatively related to relative housing prices.

Headship remains an important area for further examination. It would seem that a panel data set that explicitly follows household formation (such as the Panel Study on Income Dynamics) would provide an important vehicle for the intensive household- or nucleus-level study of headship. Headship could then be directly related to many of the important determinants of housing demand.

Decreased houshold size alone has three impacts on housing demand. The first involves per capita demand. Even in a period as long as a decade, just about half of the owner-occupiers (who now constitute about 65 percent of all U.S. households) remain in the same location. With smaller households living in the same dwelling units (and ignoring depreciation, which is low relative to the change in household size), this necessarily implies more demand per person. With the "aging" of the population, this leads to speculation about the problems of elderly living in houses that are "too big" for them, due to the transactions costs of moving, or the fear of rising prices in the face of relatively fixed retirement incomes.

Second, the new households need additional dwelling units. Standard analysis treats housing as a homogeneous commodity which can be re-shaped and re-molded. Consider, however, new household formation from children leaving their parents' homes, either as single or married heads of households. The new dwelling units require, at the very least, new kitchens and new bathrooms.

These are not generally provided by dividing the parents' (or others') homes and building the necessary rooms, but rather by the production of new units or the renovation of existing ones.

The production and renovation suggest a third impact. Increased headship probably made a considerable contribution to the decline in central city populations in the 1970s, and hence on housing demand, and on tax bases. As noted above, it is likely that existing dwelling units could not profitably meet this demand, and new dwelling units were required. Most of the available land to construct them was located outside central city limits. This discussion suggests that large fractions of the much-publicized central city population decreases (as much as 25 percent per decade in St. Louis and in Cleveland) were related to changes in household size rather than to migration of entire households. Using the identity that total population N_p is the product of number of households n_p, and average household size s_n (or $N_p = n_p s_n$), changes in population can be decomposed into *household* (number of households) effects and *size* (size of households) effects. Differentiating and re-arranging gives:

$$\hat{N}_p = \hat{n}_p + \hat{s}_n, \tag{39}$$

where *hats* refer to percentage changes. In many U.S. central cities, well over half of the population decline can be traced to the percentage fall in s_n.[45]

In city after city in the United States, numbers of households remained fairly constant, whereas declines in household size of 10 percent or more led to corrresponding drops in city population. This decline in household size is unlikely to continue at the same rate, indicating that the precipitous population declines of central city populations of the 1970s may not continue at the same rates.

4.3. Gentrification, speculation and displacement

The final market activity to be examined in the context of demographic change involves the resettlement in central (and often inner-) city neighborhoods by households that are characterized by higher incomes and differing demographics than current residents.

---

[45] Goodman [1983] performs this analysis both at the aggregate and at the neighborhood level.

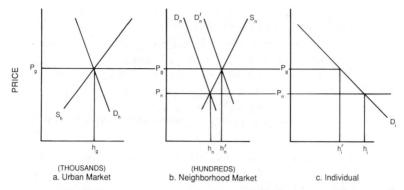

FIGURE 3   The economic impact of neighborhood gentrification.

In this process, the new (more affluent) residents bid land and housing away from current, (less affluent) residents. This inmigration has been termed "gentrification," and the bidding away of parcels has been termed "displacement." In both cases, the terminology comes largely from urban planners and geographers, and it is generally used in a pejorative sense. In a *market* sense, the inmigration and the increased prices (and possible displacement of residents) are no different from the expansion of the city outward. In urban expansion, land developers bid agricultural land away from the farmers (an activity which has also recently triggered some policy concern), in order to produce new housing.[46]

The market processes are easy to understand. Consider a neighborhood which is small compared to the rest of the city. The urban housing market is sketched in Figure 3.*a*; the neighborhood is shown in 3.*b*, and the individual within the neighborhood in 3.*c*. Neighborhood housing supply is likely to be less elastic than for the market as a whole (3.*b*), and the individual within the neighborhood takes price as parametric (3.*c*). In this analysis, housing price can be treated as rent for the renters, and as annualized rent for the owners.

For many reasons, including poor public services, bad publicity, or only-recently improved access, the prices of the housing services in the specific neighborhood (P_n) may be lower than general

---

[46] For an interesting discussion of the urbanization of agricultural land, see Fischel [1982].

market prices outside the neighborhood (P_g) and this is manifested in low home values for owners and low rents. Total housing services are represented by h_g in Figure 3.a. Since the neighborhood is small relative to the market, h_g is unchanged throughout the analysis. Neighborhood housing services are represented by h_n in Figure 3.b, determined jointly by demand D_n and supply S_n. The individual within the neighborhood purchases h_i housing services at price P_n.

Reacting to the differential between P_g and P_n, households with tastes for the type of housing offered in the neighborhood (often characterized by short commutes, specific amenities such as views of waterfronts, or unusual architecture) start to move in (demand increases in 3.b), bidding up the prices of the dwelling units to P_g. Since the supply is likely to be rather inelastic (rising from h_n to h_n'), prices may rise quickly. Landlords and home-owners in the neighborhood benefit from the influx since the capitalized value of the annualized rents increases from P_n to P_g.[47] Renters (in 3.c), who have been benefiting from below-market rents (relative to else-where), clearly suffer losses of welfare in terms of decreased housing consumption (which goes from h_i to h_i'), and decreased consumer surplus, and in some cases may be forced to move to less expensive dwellings.

Elected city officials typically land the influx as one that reverses the population decline and increases the tax base. Others, particular city planners, are concerned about the welfare loss to renters who stay, and the so-called "displacement" of those who can no longer afford their dwelling units. Since the in-movers are typically more affluent than current residents, the policy arguments are clearly those of equity, rather than efficiency, and proposed remedies vary from strict market controls, prohibiting or severely limiting the purchase of dwelling units, to aid which is targeted to displaced households. There has been little rigorous economic analysis of these effects.[48]

Studies of *gentrifiers* suggest that the process is self-limiting. Gentrifiers are often single people, childless couples, or couples

---

[47] The increased property values, and hence property taxes, may provide problems for some. In principle, this is a liquidity problem, since various types of mortgage instruments could be used to draw on the increased asset value to pay the increased taxes.

[48] See Gale [1982] for some discussion of the planning literature.

whose children are either too young or too old to use neighborhood schools. Moreover they are typically individuals with high valuation of leisure, relative to the land and public services that are more abundant and often cheaper in the suburbs. It is usually politically impossible for the administration of a large city to supply, in *specific neighborhoods* (rather than in all of them), the level of public services that would otherwise be dictated by the preferences and resources signified by higher incomes. In the vernacular of the neighborhood production function in Section 2, it is impossible to get an efficient level of public input x^k. This means that residents with tastes for the public services must either provide large amounts of private inputs, or move elsewhere, where x^k is higher.

Further evidence is consistent with this view. Studies suggest that when the household size and/or demand for services (most often schools, or child-related amenities, such as recreation or safety) grows, the households are unable to fill that demand in the gentrified neighborhood. They are either forced to purchase services outside the neighborhood (such as private schools) or to move to locations at which these services can be more easily provided.

4.4. Household level demographic characteristics

Specification of individual household behavior (in contrast ot behavior manifested through the market) is evident in three aspects of urban economics. The first aspect involves the journey-to-work, in which any realistic modeling of housing and demand (jointly determined with commuting to the job) must drop the assumption of *single worker-single workplace*. The second impact concerns the tenure choice decision, whether to own or whether to rent, which is a long run decision that is made jointly with the household size and mobility among units. The third aspect is the actual demand specification. That is, given household size and tenure choice, what are the determinants of housing demand?

4.4.1. Journey to work

It is axiomatic in modern urban economics that residential location and, by implication, housing demand are tied to the workplace location. Elsewhere in the monograph and in the series, there is substantive discussion on such location patterns. If all employment was, in fact, located downtown, then multi-worker households would have the same location decisions as single-worker households, conditional upon choosing to work (commuting and child-care costs might keep one or more of the household members out of the labor market).

The availability of jobs outside of a single central location complicates the household optimization problem immensely. One must know which (if either) worker is considered the primary worker, whether the second or secondary worker started working after locating in the house, and whether the parents anticipate changes in family size. In short, it involves optimizing an intertemporal household utility function with constraints that may include more than one income, more than one set of commuting costs, two sets of leisure time, and child care costs. It further suggests that econometric estimates of housing demand and commuting demand be jointly specified.

Little empirical work has addressed this concern. Again, this is largely due to lack of data. The AHS is a case in point. Journey-to-work data are routinely collected only with respect to the downtown area, and disclosure rules make household and job location almost impossible to determine. The Panel Study on Income Dynamics does not provide the locational data necessary for these estimates. Travel data, which often provide extensive week- or month-long travel diaries, present similar problems with respect to housing. Extensive travel data sets collected for Baltimore and Montreal, with detailed travel diaries, have contained almost no data on housing types and housing values.

The analysis above has concentrated on fixed job locations, basically ignoring the labor market and location decisions of firms. Dubin [1987] notes that if firms draw uniformly from the entire metropolitan area, the decentralization of urban jobs must increase the mean distance traveled. As a result, those workers whose family or job characteristics allow them to adjust more easily to changed job locations will have shorter commutes. More explicitly, the journey to work has both labor market and housing market components. Dubin finds that ability to adjust spatially to labor market factors may be more important than ability to adjust to housing market factors in explaining commuting to non-CBD jobs (jobs located away from downtown).

Black households have traditionally faced an additional constraint with respect to the joint commuting-housing problem. Study after study dating back to Meyer, Kain and Wohl [1964] find that, *ceteris paribus*, blacks travel greater distances and longer times to get to work. With the ending of legalized segregation and the supposed ending of legalized realtor discriminatory processes, it is harder to argue that market discrimination has a major impact. I return to this point later.

4.4.2. Tenure choice

Both the tenure choice and the housing demand decisions must involve demographic determinants. It seems apparent that bigger families need "more" housing, and the discussion above points to the jointness among household composition, commuting time, and housing purchases. Although they are jointly determined, the differences make individual discussion useful.

An earlier section of this monograph examines tenure choice in the longer term framework, and implies that the demographics are exogenous. While some demographics such as race are indeed exogenous, it is likely that households may have a longer term plan in which they decide where to live, what type of housing to purchase, whether to rent or to own, and how large a family to have. In the United States the decision to have a large [small] family (particularly since the end of World War II) is very much related to the decision to seek to own a house [rent an apartment] because owner housing usually comprises more housing. This remains true into the 1980s. Even with the large-scale conversion of apartment housing to condominium or cooperative ownership, less than 3 percent of all dwelling units are condonimiums or co-ops.

One can see the difficulty in modeling these demographic impacts, by noting how many household decisions are typically considered (in their analyses) to be exogenous.[49] As noted above, job location is explicitly assumed to be fixed. So, also, is the decision of whether (and when) to work, and the related decision as to family size. Still another decision treated as exogenous is the

---

[49] Here, tenure choice is treated simply as the decision to choose the least expensive form of housing. Lifetime wealth considerations complicate the analysis substantially.

important migration decision among cities (the *closed city–open city* question), that implies equalization of utility among urban areas. The small amount of empirical work examining sociodemographics and tenure choice explicitly, has often considered racial differences. Kain and Quigley [1975] (in a study of the 1960s St. Louis housing market) find blacks to be 9 percent less likely to own, controlling for wealth and tast parameters. Goodman [1988] finds probabilities of ownership to be unaffected by race, holding education and permanent income constant, for national samples of the late 1970s. Jones [1987] finds occupational, household size, and immigrant status to be independently important (aside from wealth considerations) in the determination of tenure choice.

As before, the theoretical modeling is probably secondary to the problems of empirical testing. The cross-sectional data sets that have typically been used are patently unsuitable for this intertemporal analysis. Even within the panel data sets that have become available, serious truncation problems remain in that *spells* of activity are not well-defined. It is useful to discuss this a bit further. Probably the most appropriate way to look at long term demographic effects at the individual level is to consider housing consumption over the spell of residence in a given unit (the term *spell* is taken from unemployment analysis; health professionals use the term *episode* similarly to refer to the period of an illness). Most housing adjustments involve the movement from one spell to the next. Any "snapshot," short of a life-time description, is necessarily truncated. Panel data, that approach the longer horizon, are essential.

4.4.3. Demand

The sections above discuss some of the theoretical problems involved in modeling demographic effects. It is appropriate, here, to discuss the types of analyses that can be used with cross-section data, involving both tenure choice and demand that is conditional on that tenure choice. This section considers methods for including demographic variables in the tenure choice and demand relationships. It also looks at the statistical problems that can occur if demographic variables are incorrectly used to model permanent income.

I then make special reference to racial variables to discuss special problems facing blacks. It is important to propose reasons why, nearly a generation after major civil rights legislation in the United States, blacks have lower housing demand that do whites. Among the reasons proposed are continued racial discrimination and/or different tastes for housing among blacks.

The last part of this section notes the importance of tastes, in general. It looks to cross cultural and survey methods as alternative means for discerning them.

a. Inclusion of demographics. Having defined criteria for an ideal model and estimation process for housing demand, it is appropriate to set up a simpler framework. Mayo [1981] is the first to discuss the lack of work in specifying demand relationships, even in the price and income variables. He finds even less consensus on the treatment of demographic variables. Consider demand H as a function of the percentage (or probability of) owning, f, the percentage (or probability of) renting, $(1-f)$, and the quantities of owner (H_o) and renter (H_r) housing.

$$H = fH_o + (1-f)H_r. \qquad (40)$$

Although owner housing is typically treated in stock terms, and renter housing in flow terms, the flow of services from owner housing is generally taken to be a constant fraction of the housing stock. Suppose further that H_o, H_r and f are all functions of income Y, price vector P, and a vector of demographic variables $\mathbf{D}$, and that at least some of the economic variables are also functions of $\mathbf{D}$. (Income, for example, might plausibly be modeled as a function of age, and education.) One can calculate an elasticity with respect to $\mathbf{D}$ of:[50]

$$\eta^*_{H\mathbf{D}} = f(H_o/H)\eta^*_{H_o\mathbf{D}} + (1-f)(H_r/H)\eta^*_{H_r\mathbf{D}} + [(H_o - H_r)/H]\eta^*_{f\mathbf{D}}. \qquad (41)$$

This *full* elasticity measures the impacts of $\mathbf{D}$ on both owner and renter demand, as well as the transition between renting and owning. Asterisks refer to *full* effects of demographic variables, both direct (in and of themselves) and indirect (through their

---

[50] All terms η_{ij} refer to the elasticity of variable i, with respect to variable j.

impacts on other variables such as permanent income). Since the average owner dwelling generally provides more services than the average renter dwelling (i.e. it has more rooms, more yard, higher quality construction; see Goodman, 1988), then the *transition* between tenure types, alone, provides a positive impact on housing demand.

The term η_{H_iD}. refers to the combined impact **D** on tenure H_i (either owning or renting), both through its own effects, and through its impact on economic variables such as permanent income. For example, a person's age may effect his or her tenure choice and/or housing demand. In addition, if permanent income is related to age (typically following a hump-backed profile), then an additional year of age, holding current income constant, changes the relationship between permanent and transitory incomes, and thus tenure choice and/or demand.

One can also derive cross-elasticities (referring, here, to the change in *elasticity,* rather than the change in quantity) of the economic (income and prices) variables with respect to **D**. Differentiating demand equation (40), first with respect to Y or P, and then to **D** yields:

$$\eta_{YD}^* = E_{oy}[\eta_{fD}^* + \eta_{H_0D}^* + \eta_{H_oyD} - \eta_{HD}^*]$$
$$+ E_{ry}[-\eta_{fD}^* + \eta_{H,D}^* + \eta_{H,yD} - \eta_{Hd}^*]$$
$$+ E_{fy}[(h_o\eta_{H_oD}^* - h_r\eta_{H,D}^*) + (h_o - h_r)(\eta_{fyD} - \eta_{HD}^*)], \quad (42a)$$

$$\eta_{PD}^* = E_{op}[\eta_{fD}^* + \eta_{H_oD}^* + \eta_{H_opD} - \eta_{HD}^*]$$
$$+ E_{rp}[-\eta_{fD}^* + \eta_{H,D}^* + \eta_{H,pD} - \eta_{HD}^*], \quad (42b)$$

where $h_o = H_o/H$, $h_r = H_r/H$, $E_{oi} = (fh_o/\mathbf{D})\eta_{H_oi}$, $E_{ri} = [(1 - f)h_r/\mathbf{D}]\eta_{H,i}$, and $E_{fi} = \eta_{fi}/\mathbf{D}$, with i referring to income or price.

From the model, demographic variables can affect owner demand, renter demand, or the transition probability (which will affect demand on the premise that owner housing provides more housing than does renter housing).[51] However, the transition probability does not enter the cross-price elasticity (42b) if both owner and renter housing prices increase by the same percentage,

---

[51] This need not be the case, although it seems to typify most Western housing markets.

and if the tenure choice (as assumed in this derivation) is homogeneous in relative prices.

This suggests estimation procedures that allow these cross-elasticities to differ from 0, and indicates that routine use of logarithmic transformations is particularly inappropriate. Consider a generalized demand function:

$$(H^{\kappa_0} - 1)/\kappa_0 = \beta_0 + \beta_1(Y^{\kappa_1} - 1)/\kappa_1$$
$$+ \beta_2(P^{\kappa_2} - 1)/\kappa_2 + \beta_3(D^{\kappa_3} - 1)/\kappa_3 + \varepsilon. \quad (43)$$

This function subsumes both linear and logarithmic forms, since the limit of $(x_i^{\kappa_i} - 1)/\kappa_i$, as $\kappa_i \to 0$, is (through l'Hôpital's rule) $\ln x_i$. Income, price and demographic elasticities (respectively) are:

$$\eta_Y = \beta_1 Y^{\kappa_1} H^{-\kappa_0}, \quad \eta_P = \beta_2 Y^{\kappa_2} H^{-\kappa_0}, \quad \text{and} \quad \eta_D = \beta_3 D^{\kappa_3} H^{-\kappa_0}. \quad (44)$$

The cross-elasticity of income elasticity with respect to D, for example, is:

$$\eta_{YD} = (\partial \eta_Y / \partial D)(D/\eta_Y) = -\kappa_0 \eta_D. \quad (45)$$

If κ_0 is constrained to 0 (logarithmic form), all cross elasticities are likewise constrained to be zero.

Recent literature on the specification of demographic variables has proceeded from a utility maximization framework into the estimation of demand systems (for example, Pollak and Wales, 1981 or Gorman, 1976). Techniques involve *translation* (changing the origin) by demographic variables, *scaling* (finding the appropriate demographic multiple[s]) and combinations of the two (often referred to as "Gorman" methods). The joint estimation of the interaction of demographic variables on both demand and tenure choice has not been explicitly treated.

The abundance of household-level data sets over the past 20 years (as well as the requisite hardware and software to handle them) has enabled researchers to refine household-level estimates. Econometricians are now able to estimate behavioral parameters directly from individuals, rather than from the aggregates that were previously used. As noted above, some demographic impacts, such as age (though a life-cycle income format), or household size, can be deduced from the standard constrained utility model.

Yet, even the specification of those variables which are handled well in theory can present substantive empirical problems. Early attempts to implement permanent income in demand analyses involved inclusion of socioeconomic characteristics along with current income to control for the supposed determinants of permanent income.

$$H = \sum_i \omega_i d_i + \alpha Y + e. \qquad (46a)$$

Coefficient α of (46a) was then interpreted as a permanent income elasticity.

More recent methods have regressed current income Y on a set of sociodemographic variables, using the predicted value for the household as permanent income, and the residual as transitory income. Both Cameron [1986] and Goodman [1988] reveal a major flaw in the analysis typified by (46a). Suppose that housing demand is a function only of permanent (Y^P) and transitory (Y^T) incomes, such that:

$$H = \alpha_P Y^P + \alpha_T Y^T + u. \qquad (46b)$$

Assume that $Y^P = \sum_i \beta_i d_i$, and $Y = Y^P + Y^T$. Substitution and rearrangement of (46b), with current income Y and the demographic variables d_i reveals:

$$H = \sum_I (\alpha_P - \alpha_T)\beta_i d_i + \alpha_T Y + e. \qquad (46c)$$

The resulting regression is mathematically identical to (46a). The income coefficient on (46c) equals α_T, which is the same coefficient α that is estimated in (46a). Thus the misspecified regression identifies the *transitory* income coefficient (the coefficient of Y), rather than the permanent income *or* the current income coefficient. Although this is admittedly a simplified case, it shows the likelihood that many studies which have reported low income elasticities have had this flaw.

In addition, some reconciliation between cross-section and panel data is necessary. Panel data permit estimation of many household level *fixed effects* that can not be handled with cross-section data. Börsch-Supan [1988] recognizes the necessity of correcting for household-specific effects that are revealed using panel data. Using the Panel Study on Income Dynamics, he finds that standard cross-section studies overestimate price and income elasticities, and underestimate the importance of demographic factors.

b. Racial factors. Still another example of problems with de-mographic variables involves the measurement of housing market discrimination. A major impetus to the development of urban economics as a separate field involved the analysis and measure-ment of racial discrimination in urban housing and labor markets. It has become clear that housing market discrimination (usually against blacks) can only properly be discerned at the household level.[52] As noted in Section 4.4.2, early studies such as Kain and Quigley [1975] find that, all else equal, blacks were less likely to own in St. Louis in the 1960s. Goodman and Kawai [1982] find that New Haven black owners purchase less housing than comparable whites in the late 1960s. Goodman [1988] finds lower black housing consumption in the late 1970s for both owner and renter housing, even though at most income levels, controlling for permanent income, blacks are *more* likely to own than whites. These studies, controlling to the greatest extent possible with cross-section data, suggest that either discrimination, in some form, or differing tastes for housing relative to other goods, provide explanations.

Is it possible that, over 20 years after the legal abolition of the last institutionalized housing discrimination practices, the differentials in observed housing purchases are still related to discriminatory practices by sellers, realtors and lenders? In a very careful study based on *Fair Housing Audits,* Yinger [1986] provides evidence that would suggest an affirmative answer. In these audits (undertaken in Boston in 1981), individuals from the white majority were matched with minority individuals based on various socioeconomic characteristics. Both groups then visited landlords or real estate brokers in search of housing. Statistical analysis (paired difference-of-means) was then used to estimate and to infer the existence and/or extent of racial discrimination using these matched pairs.

Yinger finds that black auditors are invited to see 36.3 percent fewer apartments than are white counterparts. Racial discrimination does not seem to vary according to black characteristics, although there seem to be discriminatory aspects toward showing houses for sale to low income blacks. Discrimination is particularly salient with

---

[52] Many early studies confounded neighborhood market effects, with discrimina-tion toward individuals. Yinger [1979] still provides the best comparative discussion of differing models of housing market discrimination.

respect to neighborhood characteristics, in that there is substantial discrimination in white neighborhoods, and little discrimination in black neighborhoods.

It is also worth discussing whether *pure* demographic characteristics may affect housing demand. In terms of the black population, it is useful to consider whether (irrespective of current practices) a legacy of housing market discrimination may have influenced black tastes for housing by decreasing expectations. This suggests more aggressive examination of tastes in the determination of housing demand.

c. Tastes. Economists have often been content to leave the characterization and measurement of tastes to other disciplines. The distinction (especially in the micro-economic theory) between tastes (taken as given) and "economic" variables, enables them to treat the impacts of income and price changes as the sole determinants of changes in purchases.

Two additional types of analyses for isolating tastes may be helpful. *Economic historians* have traditionally utilized international comparisons between recent immigrants to a new country and those who stayed in the native country. This analysis uses the premise that while the environment may have changed, the tastes, as they are understood, might have remained constant.

The second possibility involves *survey methods,* using hypothetical alternatives. Economists have been skeptical of such research, feeling that surveys may not provide either realistic possibilities or explicit price or income constraints, and do not impose the costs of making wrong decisions. A growing environmental literature shows that improved techniques lead to plausible results in the valuation of environmental amenities. Such methods may provide useful information for housing analysts in identifying utility (or compensated demand) functions apart from market imperfections (such as costly adjustment, or racial discrimination) that may constrain choices.

4.5. Discussion

It is apparent that demographic variables can have major impacts on the analyses of housing markets. Variables such as population size and numbers of households, and by implication, household size, can affect the modeling of city size, and the movement into and out of neighborhoods. Still another aspect of this discussion is the *age structure* of the population. With the cohorts of population over the ages of 65 (and 75 and 85) growing at unprecedented rates, and demanding different types of housing, the ability to predict and to meet the changed housing demand will have major theoretical and policy implications. One can use general trends to derive macroeconomic projections of housing needs for the elderly, but it is much more difficult to estimate the demand within a metropolitan area, given the current locations of the elderly, and the amounts and types of housing stock necessary to serve them.

It is clear that the household-level modeling should be done with a life-cycle approach where family size, workplace location (and by implication leisure time), savings and housing demand are jointly determined. The theory involves the simultaneous optimization of these factors, and even assuming perfect foresight, the solutions are complicated. The empirical work is even more difficult, requiring panel data for households, and sophisticated econometric modeling techniques that mix discrete choices (such as owning *v.* renting, or forming a household) with continuous ones (such as housing demand).

Finally, economists should examine how the demographic characteristics reflect tastes. Work thus far has largely modeled demographics in terms of differential nonmarket productivity. Hence, a husband and wife may choose different values of leisure time because one is relatively more productive in the home than in the office. Such analyses may be valid, yet it is also clear that tastes for various goods may vary according to sociodemographic factors. These relationships should be studied more intensively.

5. CONCLUSIONS AND OBSERVATIONS

This monograph has examined three current topics in empirical housing analysis:

1) Neighborhood effects.

2) Short run and long run equilibrium.

3) Demographic variables.

Each has both theoretical and empirical implications both for the "truth and beauty" of economic analysis, as well as for the formulation and the implementation of economic policy. Each suffers not only from theoretical modeling problems, but also from data inadequacies, for the proper testing of the models.

Since much of the discussion addresses data considerations, it is useful to summarize the availability and quality of data for the urban economic analysis, before looking once more at the three individual topics. In each case, I recapitulate the research needs related both to theoretical and empirical analysis.

5.1. Urban housing data

The evolution of large mainframe computers, high density media, and inexpensive personal computing resources over the past twenty years, has permitted a level of data analysis that would have previously been inconceivable. The availability of large disaggregated data sets and the sophisticated hardware and software for handling them has not only improved the analysis, but has revealed the inadequacies of both theoretical and econometric models.

Housing demand is a case in point. Up to the mid 1970s, state of the art analyses placed housing expenditures (in logarithmic form) on the left hand side of the equation, and income (also in logarithmic form) on the right hand side. Price was hard to measure and was often omitted. The resulting income elasticities were then estimated and accepted. Since then, analysts have come to realize that housing demand is jointly determined with tenure choice, family size, mobility within metropolitan areas, and migration among them. The theoretical and econometric models have proceeded and advanced together.

Many data sets have been extraordinarily useful to housing researchers. The two most widely used sources are the American Housing Survey and the Panel Study on Income Dynamics, but both lack good geographic detail, and good tax information that would be useful for determining marginal tax rates, and hence housing user costs. Analysts who collect or compile their own data must address these concerns, since the geographic detail is important for neighborhood considerations and the tax information is an important aspect of household resource allocation.

5.2. Neighborhood effects

The first topic in the monograph was the importance and analysis of neighborhood effects. *Neighborhood* interacts crucially with both housing demand and housing supply. Failure to model neighborhood properly leads to substantive errors in considering both the individual and the market level behavior.

Two approaches should be addressed with respect to theory. First, the treatment of neighborhood as a *quasi-public good* is important in understanding the provision of neighborhood attributes. It should be considered, if possible, in both the closed-form analytical work and in urban housing simulation models. Second, neighborhood should also be included is the general equilibrium analysis of the *closed-city* models which are vital in measuring the impacts of amenity improvements. The overlapping neighborhoods model is an important innovation, and should be examined more fully.

Empirically, it is necessary to examine the measurement of neighborhood effects through both housing price and quantity adjustments. Rigorous comparison of the hedonic price or discrete choice models will also be quite useful. Given the arbitrary nature of any set of neighborhood boundaries, more understanding of spatial autocorrelation is also essential.

Census indicators at the block, block group, and census tract levels are likely to remain the the best neighborhood indicators. Census data are collected only every 10 years, and released slowly. For example, detailed data from the 1980 Census were not readily available until 1983. Further, current Census Bureau plans suggest cutbacks in the number of indicators to be surveyed for 1990. Nonetheless, they are collected according to the same criteria in all metropolitan areas, and are generally comparable within and among the metropolitan areas.

5.3. The long run and short run

The high transactions costs that accompany the purchase and sale of housing services suggest that single period optimization models are inadequate both theoretically and empirically. It is apparent that households optimize over the long term, and that the resulting efficiency conditions differ substantially from the short term conditions. Econometric examination of the specification errors from single period optimization indicates that the single-period models lead to inconsistent estimates. Both theoretical and econometric modeling must then consider the multi-period nature of the optimization.

The analytics of intertemporal optimization are fairly well understood, but the major theoretical efforts must occur in the modeling of both household and landlord expectations. Theoretical models alternatively assume current-period myopia, or perfect life-time foresight. Little theoretical or empriical work has adequately considered the formulation of expectations, yet it is clear that such expectations drive the long term decision-making processes of these actors.

The theoretical modeling must accompany the collection and maintenance of panel data sets. The Panel Study on Income Dynamics would constitute the best source for consumer expectations. The American Housing Survey is possibly the only panel data set available for suppliers, although the EHAP Supply Experiment data may also provide useful landlord information.

5.4. Demographic variables

Like many other economic fields, housing analyses have largely ignored demographic considerations. Yet, it is clear that many aspects of housing market behavior, such as population decentralization, neighborhood gentrification, and, of course, racial discrimination, are driven by demographic factors. Economists have left much of the recent analyses to planners and geographers. Urban economics can offer considerable insights into the effects of demographics on these housing market activities.

It is also important to consider the household demographic effects in a model (as sketched out in Section 5.1) that makes the demographics endogenous. The joint modeling of housing demand with family formation represents a line of analysis that should be strengthened. This research agenda may have important policy implications, particularly with reference to the aging of the population, and its impact on housing demand, housing supply, and the resulting urban structure.

Finally, methods from other fields of the discipline may provide useful insights. Cross-cultural research, as performed by economic historians and development economists, may yield information on tastes, separated from the specific environment. Experimental methods and survey research may also be helpful in distinguishing tastes from other demographic factors.

5.5. Empirical housing analysis

Housing analysis has represented a field in which microeconomic and microeconometric methods are applied to problems that have theoretical, empirical, and policy implications. The three topics outlined in the monograph require extensions of the theoretical and empirical modeling. The treatment of neighborhood externalities, the modeling of intertemporal choice, and the analysis of household demographics constitute exciting and important parts of the urban housing economics research agenda. They have important implications, as well, for the formulation and evaluation of housing policy.

Acknowledgments

Professor of Economics, Wayne State University, Detroit, MI 48202. I am grateful to Richard Arnott, Axel Börsch-Supan, Edward Coulson, Robin Dubin, Janet Hankin, Richard Muth, and Peter Zorn for comments and suggestions.

References

[1] Alonso, W., *Location and Land Use,* Cambridge, MA: Harvard University Press, 1964.
[2] Anas, A., "A Model of Residential Change and Neighborhood Tipping," *Journal of Urban Economics* 7 (May 1980): 358–70.
[3] Anas, A., *Residential Location Markets and Urban Transportation,* New York: Academic Press, 1982.
[4] Anas, A., "Modelling in Urban and Regional Economics," in J. Lesourne and H. Sonnenschein, Eds., *Fundamals of Pure and Applied Economics and Encyclopaedia of Economics,* Paris: Harwood, 1987.
[5] Anderson, J. E., "Ridge Estimation of House Value Determinants," *Journal of Urban Economics* 9 (May 1981): 286–97.
[6] Arnott, R., D. Pines, and E. Sadka, "The Effects of an Equiproportional Transport Improvement in a Fully-Closed Monocentric City," *Regional Science and Urban Economics* 16 (August 1966): 387–406.
[7] Bailey, M. J., "Note on the Economics of Residential Zoning and Urban Renewal," *Land Economics* 35 (August 1957): 288–92.

138   ALLEN C. GOODMAN

[8] Bartik, T. J. and V. K. Smith, "Urban Amenities and Public Policy," in *Handbook of Urban Economics*, (E. S. Mills, Ed.), Amsterdam: North-Holland 1987.

[9] Becker, G. S., *The Economics of Discrimination*, Chicago: The University of Chicago Press, 1957.

[10] Becker, G. S., "A Theory on the Allocation of Time," *Economic Journal* 75 (September 1965): 493–517.

[11] Börsch-Supan, A., "On the West German Tenants' Protection Legislation," *Journal of Institutional and Theoretical Economics* 142 (June 1986): 380–404.

[12] Börsch-Supan, A., "Economic Analysis of Discrete Choice," *Lecture Notes in Economics and Mathematical Systems*, Berlin: Springer-Verlag, 1987.

[13] Bradbury, K. and A. Downs, *Do Housing Allowances Work?*, Washington: Brookings, 1982.

[14] Cameron, T. A., "Permanent and Transitory Income in a Model of Housing Demand," *Journal of Urban Economics* 20 (September 1986): 205–10.

[15] Courant, P. N. and J. M. Yinger, "On Models of Racial Prejudice and Urban Residential Structure," *Journal of Urban Economics* 4 (July 1977): 272–91.

[16] Davis, O. A., and A. B. Whinston, "Economics of Urban Renewal," *Law and Contemporary Problems* 26 (Winter 1961): 105–17.

[17] Deleeuw, F., "The Demand for Housing: A Review of the Cross-Section Evidence," *Review of Economics and Statistics* 53 (February 1972): 1–10.

[18] Deleeuw, F. and R. J. Struyk, *The Web of Housing*, Washington: Urban Institute, 1976.

[19] Dhrymes, P. J., *Econometrics*, New York: Harper and Row, 1970.

[20] Dougherty, A. and R. Van Order, "Inflation, Housing Costs, and the Consumer Price Index," *American Economic Review* 72 (March 1982): 154–64.

[21] Dubin, R. A., "Commuting Patterns and Firm Decentralization," Wayne State University, manuscript, 1987.

[22] Dubin, R. A., "Estimating the Effects of Spatial Autocorrelation with Maximum Likelihood Methods," *Review of Economics and Statistics*, forthcoming, 1988.

[23] Dubin, R. A. and A. C. Goodman, "Valuation of Education and Crime Neighborhood Characteristics Through Hedonic Housing Prices," *Population and Environment* 5 (Fall 1982): 166–81.

[24] Dynarski, M., "The Economics of Community: Theory and Measurement," Ph.D. Dissertation, The Johns Hopkins University, 1981.

[25] Engle, R. F. and R. C. Marshall, "A Microeconomic Analysis of Vacant Housing Units," in *The Urban Economy and Housing*, (R. Grieson, Ed.), Lexington, MA: D. C. Heath, 1983.

[26] Ellickson, B. C., "An Alternative Test of the Hedonic Theory of Housing Markets," *Journal of Urban Economics* 9 (January 1981): 56–79.

[27] Epple, D., "Hedonic Prices and Implicit Markets: Estimating Demand and Supply Functions for Differentiated Products," *Journal of Political Economy* 95 (February 1987): 59–80.

[28] Fischel, W. A., "The Urbanization of Agricultural Land: A Review of the National Agricultural Lands Study," *Land Economics* 58 (May 1982): 236–59.

[29] Follain, J. R., "The Price Elasticity of Long-Run Supply of New Housing Construction," *Land Economics* 55 (May 1979): 190–9.

[30] Follain, J. R. and S. Malpezzi, "Dissecting Housing Value and Rent," Washington: Urban Institute, 1980.

[31] Freeman, A. M., "Hedonic Prices, Property Values and Measuring Environmental Benefits: A Survey of the Issues," *Scandinavian Journal of Economics* **81** (Vol. 2, 1979): 154–73.
[32] Friedman, J. and D. H. Weinberg, *The Economics of Housing Vouchers,* New York: Academic Press, 1982.
[33] Friedman, M., *A Theory of the Consumption Function,* Princeton, NJ: Princeton University Press, 1957.
[34] Fujita, M., "Urban Land Use Theory," in J. Lesourne and H. Sonnenschein, Eds., *Fundamentals of Pure and Applied Economics and Encyclopaedia of Economics* Paris: Harwood, 1987.
[35] Gale, D., *Neighborhood Revitalization and the Postindustrial City,* Lexington, MA: D. C. Heath, 1982.
[36] Goodman, A. C., "Hedonic Prices, Prices Indices and Housing Markets," *Journal of Urban Economics* **5** (October 1978): 471–84.
[37] Goodman, A. C., "Household Size and Population Size: A Tract Level Analysis," Census Note 6, Center for Metropolitan Planning and Research, The Johns Hopkins University, 1982.
[38] Goodman, A. C., "Demographics of Individual Housing Demand," Wayne State University, manuscript, 1988.
[39] Goodman, A. C., "An Econometric Model of Housing Price, Permanent Income, Tenure Choice, and Housing Demand," *Journal of Urban Economics,* **23** (May 1988): 227–53.
[40] Goodman, A. C. and M. Kawai, "Permanent Income, Hedonic Prices and Housing Demand: New Evidence," *Journal of Urban Economics* **12** (September 1982): 214–37.
[41] Goodman, A. C. and M. Kawai, "Replicative Evidence on Rental and Owner Demand for Housing," *Southern Economic Journal* **50** (April 1984): 1036–57.
[42] Goodman, A. C. and M. Kawai, "Length of Residence Discounts and Renter Housing Demand: Theory and Evidence," *Land Economics* **61** (May 1985): 93–105.
[43] Goodman, A. C. and M. Kawai, "Functional Form, Sample Selection and Housing Demand," *Journal of Urban Economics* **20** (September 1986): 155–67.
[44] Goodman, A. C. and R. B. Taylor, *The Baltimore Neighborhood Factbook,* Center for Metropolitan Planning and Research, The Johns Hopkins University, 1983.
[45] Gorman, W. M., "Tricks with Utility Functions," in *Essays in Economic Analysis,* (M. J. Artis, and A. R. Nobay, Eds.), Cambridge: Cambridge University Press, 1976.
[46] Griliches, Z., "Hedonic Prices Revisited," in *Price Indexes and Quality Change* (Z. Griliches, Ed.), Cambridge, MA: Harvard University Press, 1971: 3–15.
[47] Gronau, R., "The Intrafamily Allocation of Time: The Value of the Housewives' Time," *American Economic Review* **68** (September 1973): 634–51.
[48] Gronau, R., "Leisure, Home Production and Work—The Theory of the Allocation of Time Revisited," *Journal of Political Economy* **85** (December 1977) 1099–1123.
[49] Guest, A., "Residential Segregation in Urban Areas," in *Contemporary Topics in Urban Sociology,* (K. P. Schwirian Ed.), Morristown, NJ: General Learning Press, 1977.

[50] Hanushek, E. A. and J. M. Quigley, "What is the Price Elasticity of Housing Demand," *Review of Economics and Statistics* 61 (November 1979): 449–54.
[51] Harrison, D., and D. L. Rubinfeld, "The Air Pollution and Property Value Debate: Some Empirical Evidence," *Review of Economics and Statistics* 60 (November 1978): 635–8.
[52] Heckman, J. J., "Sample Selection Bias as a Specification Error," *Econometrica* 47 (January 1979): 153–61.
[53] Henderson, J. V. and Y. M. Ioannides, "Dynamic Aspects of Consumer Decisions in Housing Markets," Brown University Working Paper 84–36.
✓ [54] Hirsch, W. Z., *Urban Economics*, New York: MacMillan Publishing Company, 1984, Ch. 9.
[55] Hirshleifer, J., *Price Theory and Its Applications,* Englewood Cliffs, NJ: Prentice-Hall, Inc., 1976, Chapter 8.
[56] Hochman, O. and H. Ofek, "The Value of Time in Consumption and Residential Location in an Urban Setting," *American Economic Review* 67 (December 1977): 996–1003.
[57] Hoyt, H., *The Structure and Growth of Residential Neighborhoods in American Cities,* Washington: Federal Housing Administration, 1939.
[58] Jones, L. D., "Household Wealth and Tenure Choice," Center for Real Estate Research, The University of California, Berkeley, manuscript, 1987.
[59] Kain, J. F., "Housing Segregation, Negro Employment, and Metropolitan Decentralization," *Quarterly Journal of Economics* 82 (May 1968): 175–97.
[60] Kain, J. F. and J. M. Quigley, *Housing Markets and Racial Discrimination,* New York: Columbia University Press, 1975.
[61] Kanemoto, Y., "Externalities in Space," in J. Lesourne and H. Sonnenschein, Eds., *Fundamentals of Pure and Applied Economics and Encyclopaedia of Economics,* Paris: Harwood, 1987.
[62] King, A. T., *Property Taxes, Amenities, and Residential Land Values,* Cambridge, MA: Ballinger, 1973.
[63] Lapham, V., "Do Blacks Pay More for Housing?" *Journal of Political Economy* 79 (November/December 1971): 1244–57.
[64] Lancaster, K. J., "A New Approach to Consumer Theory," *Journal of Political Economy* 74 (April 1966): 132–57.
[65] Lind, R. C., "Spatial Equilibrium, Rents, and Public Program Benefits," *Quarterly Journal of Economics* 87 (May 1973): 188–207.
[66] Little, J. T., "Residential Preferences, Neighborhood Filtering and Neighborhood Change," *Journal of Urban Economics* 3 (January 1976): 68–81.
[67] Lösch, A., *The Economics of Location,* New Haven: Yale University Press, 1954.
[68] Loury, G. C., "The Minimum Border Hypothesis Does Not Explain the Shape of Black Ghettos," *Journal of Urban Economics* 5 (April 1978): 147–53.
[69] Lowry, I. S. "Rental Housing in the 1970s: Searching for the Crisis," in *Rental Housing: Is There A Crisis?,* (J. C. Weicher, K. E. Villani, and E. A. Roistacher, Eds.), Washington: Urban Institute Press, 1981.
[70] Maddala, G. S., *Limited Dependent and Qualitative Variables in Econometrics,* New York: Cambridge University Press, 1983.
[71] Marshall, R. C. and J. L. Gúasch, "Occupancy Discounts in the U.S. Rental Housing Market," *Oxford Bulletin of Economics and Statistics* 45 (November 1983): 357–78.
[72] Mayer, N. S., "The Impacts of Lending, Race, and Ownership on Rental Housing Rehabilitation," *Journal of Urban Economics* 17 (May 1985): 349–74.

[73] Mayo, S. K., "Theory and Estimation in the Economics of Housing Demand," *Journal of Urban Economics* **10** (July 1981): 95–116.
[74] McDonald, J. F., *Economic Analysis of An Urban Housing Market,* New York: Academic Press, 1979.
[75] McFadden, D., "Conditional Logit Analysis of Qualitative Choice Behavior," in *Frontiers in Econometrics,* (P. Zarembka, Ed.), 1974.
[76] McFadden, D., "Modeling the Choice of Residential Location," in *Spatial Interaction Theory and Residential Location,* (A. Karlquist et al., Eds.), Amsterdam: North-Holland, 1978.
[77] Meyer, J. R., J. F. Kain and M. Wohl. *The Urban Transportation Problem,* Cambridge, MA: Harvard University Press, 1965.
[78] Mieszkowski, P. and M. Straszheim, *Current Issues in Urban Economics,* Baltimore: Johns Hopkins Press, 1979.
[79] Mills, E. S., *Studies in the Structure of the Urban Economy,* Baltimore: Johns Hopkins Press, 1972.
[80] Mills, E. S., Ed., *Handbook of Urban Economics,* Amsterdam; North-Holland, 1987).
[81] Mills, E. S. and B. W. Hamilton, *Urban Economics,* New York: Scott Foresman, 1984.
[82] Miyao, T., "Urban Growth and Dynamics," in J. Lesourne and H. Sonnenschein, Eds., *Fundamentals of Pure and Applied Economics and Encyclopaedia of Economics,* Paris: Harwood, 1987.
[83] Muth, R. F., "The Demand for Nonfarm Housing," in *The Demand for Durable Goods,* (A. Harburger, Ed.), Chicago: University of Chicago Press, 1960, 29–96.
[84] Muth, R. F., "Urban Residential Land and Housing Markets," in *Issues in Urban Economics,* (H. S. Perloff and L. Wingo Jr, Eds.), Baltimore: Johns Hopkins University Press, 1968, 285–334.
[85] Muth, R. F., *Cities and Housing,* Chicago: University of Chicago Press, 1969.
[86] Muth, R. F., "Moving Costs and Housing Expenditures," *Journal of Urban Economics* **1** (January 1974): 108–25.
[87] Olsen, E. O., "Housing Programs and the Forgotten Taxpayer," *The Public Interest* **66** (Winter 1982): 97–109.
[88] Olsen, E. O., "Demand and Supply of Housing Services," in *Handbook of Urban Economics,* (E. S. Mills, Ed.), Amsterdam: North-Holland, 1987.
[89] Ozanne, L. J. and R. J. Struyk, "The Price Elasticity of Supply of Housing Services," in *Urban Housing Markets: Recent Directions in Research and Policy,* (L. S. Bourne and J. R. Hitchcock, Eds.), Toronto: University of Toronto Press, 1978.
[90] Park, R. E. and E. W. Burgess, *The City,* Chicago: University of Chicago Press, 1925.
[91] Plaut, S. E., "The Timing of Housing Tenure Transition," *Journal of Urban Economics* **21** (May 1987): 312–22.
[92] Polinsky, A. M., "The Demand for Housing: A Study in Specification and Grouping," *Econometrica* **45** (March 1977): 447–61.
[93] Polinsky, A. M. and D. T. Ellwood, "An Empirical Reconciliation of Micro and Grouped Estimates of the Demand for Housing," *Review of Economics and Statistics* **61** (May 1979): 199–205.
[94] Polinsky, A. M. and S. Shavell, "Amenities and Property Values in a Model of an Urban Area," *Journal of Public Economics* **5** (January/February 1976): 119–30.

[95] Pollak, R. A. and T. J. Wales, "Demographic Variables in Demand Analysis," *Econometrica* **49** (November 1981): 1533–51.

[96] Porell, F. W., "One Man's Ceiling is Another Man's Floor: Landlord/Manager Residency and Housing Conditon," *Land Economics* **61** (May 1985): 106–18.

[97] Quigley, J. M., "What Have We Learned About Urban Housing Markets?" in *Current Issues in Urban Economics*, (P. Mieszkowski and M. Straszheim, Eds.), Baltimore: Johns Hopkins Press, 1979.

[98] Quigley, J. M., "Estimates of a More General Model of Consumer Choice in the Housing Market," in *The Urban Economy and Housing*, (R. E. Grieson, Ed.), Lexington, MA: D. C. Heath, 1983.

[99] Quigely, J. M. and D. H. Weinberg, "Intra-urban Residential Mobility: A Review and Synthesis," *International Regional Science Review* **2** (Spring 1977): 41–66.

[100] Reid, M. G., *Housing and Income*, Chicago: University of Chicago Press, 1962.

[101] Rosen, H. S., "Housing Decisions and the U.S. Income Tax: An Econometric Analysis, *Journal of Public Economics*, **11** (February 1979): 1–24.

[102] Rosen, S. "Hedonic Prices and Implicit Markets: Product Differentiation in Pure Competition," *Journal of Political Economy* **82** (February 1974): 34–55.

[103] Rossi, P. H. and A. B. Shlay, "Residential Mobility and Public Policy Issues: 'Why Families Move' Revisited," *Journal of Social Issues* **38** (Fall 1982): 21–34.

[104] Schelling, T. C., "On the Ecology of Micro-Motives," *The Public Interest* **25** (Fall 1971): 59–98.

[105] Shelton, J. P., "The Cost of Renting Vs. Owning a House," *Land Economics* **44** (February 1968): 59–72.

[106] Smith, L. B., "Household Headship Rates, Household Formation, and Housing Demand in Canada," *Land Economics* **60** (May 1984): 180–88.

[107] Starr, R., "An End to Rental Housing," *The Public Interest* **57** (Fall 1979): 25–38.

[108] Sternlieb, G., *The Tenement Landlord*, New Brunswick: Rutgers University Press, 1969.

[109] Stover, M. E., "The Price Elasticity of the Supply of Single-Family Detached Urban Housing," *Journal of Urban Economics* **20** (November 1986): 331–40.

[110] Strange, W., "Overlapping Neighborhoods and Housing Externalities," University of British Columbia, manuscript, 1987.

[111] Taeuber, K. E. and A. F. Taeuber, *Negroes in Cities*, Chicago: Aldine, 1965.

[112] Tiebout, C. M., "A Pure Theory of Local Expenditures," *Journal of Political Economy* **64** (October 1956): 416–24.

[113] Von Thünen, J. H., *Der Isolierte Staat in Beziehung auf Landwirtschaft und Nationalokonomie*, Hamburg.

[114] Wheaton, W. C., "Monocentric Models of Urban Land Use," in *Current Issues in Urban Economics*, (P. Mieszkowski and M. Straszheim, Eds.), Baltimore: Johns Hopkins Press, 1979.

[115] White, M. J., "A Model of Residential Location Choice and Commuting by Men and Women Workers," *Journal of Regional Science* **17** (February 1977): 41–52.

[116] White, M. J., "Government Response to Spending Limitations," *National Tax Journal* **32** Supplement (June 1979): 201–9.

[117] Yinger, J. M., "A Note on the Length of the Black-White Border," *Journal of Urban Economics* **3** (October 1976): 370–82.

[118] Yinger, J. M., "Prejudice and Discrimination in the Urban Housing Market," in *Current Issues in Urban Economics,* (P. Mieszkowski and M. Straszheim, Eds.), Baltimore: Johns Hopkins University Press, 1979.
[119] Yinger, J. M., "Measuring Racial Discrimination with Fair Housing Audits," *American Economic Review* **76** (December 1986): 881–93.
[120] Zorn, P. M., "Capitalization, Population Movement, and the Local Public Sector: A Probabilistic Analysis," *Journal of Urban Economics* **17** (March 1985): 189–207.

AUTHOR INDEX

SUBJECT INDEX

147

FUNDAMENTALS OF PURE AND APPLIED ECONOMICS

SECTIONS AND EDITORS

BALANCE OF PAYMENTS AND INTERNATIONAL FINANCE
W. Branson, Princeton University

DISTRIBUTION
A. Atkinson, London School of Economics

ECONOMIC DEMOGRAPHY
T.P. Schultz, Yale University

ECONOMIC DEVELOPMENT STUDIES
S. Chakravarty, Delhi School of Economics

ECONOMIC FLUCTUATIONS: FORECASTING, STABILIZATION, INFLATION, SHORT TERM MODELS, UNEMPLOYMENT
A. Ando, University of Pennsylvania

ECONOMIC HISTORY
P. David, Stanford University, and M. Lévy-Leboyer, Université Paris X

ECONOMIC SYSTEMS
J.M. Montias, Yale University, and J. Kornai, Institute of Economics, Hungarian Academy of Sciences

ECONOMICS OF HEALTH, EDUCATION, POVERTY AND CRIME
V. Fuchs, Stanford University

ECONOMICS OF THE HOUSEHOLD AND INDIVIDUAL BEHAVIOR
J. Muellbauer, University of Oxford

ECONOMICS OF TECHNOLOGICAL CHANGE
F. M. Scherer, Swarthmore College

ECONOMICS OF UNCERTAINTY AND INFORMATION
S. Grossman, Princeton University, and J. Stiglitz, Princeton University

EVOLUTION OF ECONOMIC STRUCTURES, LONG-TERM MODELS, PLANNING POLICY, INTERNATIONAL ECONOMIC STRUCTURES
W. Michalski, O.E.C.D., Paris

EXPERIMENTAL ECONOMICS
C. Plott, California Institute of Technology

GAME THEORY
R. Aumann, The Hebrew University of Jerusalem

GENERAL EQUILIBRIUM THEORY AND OPTIMUM THEORY
W. Hildenbrand, University of Bonn, and A. Mas-Colell, Harvard University

GOVERNMENT OWNERSHIP AND REGULATION OF ECONOMIC
ACTIVITY
E. Bailey, Carnegie-Mellon University

INTERNATIONAL ECONOMIC ISSUES
T. Fujii, University of Nagoya

INTERNATIONAL TRADE
M. Kemp, University of New South Wales

LABOR ECONOMICS
F. Welch, University of California, Los Angeles

LAW AND ECONOMICS
S. Shavell, Harvard Law School

MACROECONOMIC THEORY
J. Grandmont, CEPREMAP

MARXIAN ECONOMICS
J. Roemer, University of California, Davis

MONETARY THEORY
N. Wallace, University of Minnesota

NATURAL RESOURCES AND ENVIRONMENTAL ECONOMICS
C. Henry, Ecole Polytechnique, Paris

ORGANIZATION THEORY AND ALLOCATION PROCESSES
A. Postlewaite, University of Pennsylvania, and D. Schmeidler,
Tel Aviv University

POLITICAL SCIENCE AND ECONOMICS
J. Ferejohn, Stanford University

PROGRAMMING METHODS IN ECONOMICS
M. Balinski, Ecole Polytechnique, Paris

PUBLIC EXPENDITURES
P. Dasgupta, University of Oxford

REGIONAL AND URBAN ECONOMICS
R. Arnott, Queen's University at Kingston

SOCIAL CHOICE THEORY
A. Sen, University of Oxford

TAXES
R. Guesnerie, Ecole des Hautes Etudes en Sciences Sociales

THEORY OF ECONOMIC GROWTH
J. Scheinkman, University of Chicago

THEORY OF THE FIRM AND INDUSTRIAL ORGANIZATION
A. Jacquemin, Université Catholique de Louvain

PUBLISHED TITLES

Further titles in preparation
ISSN: 0191-1708